Living M/s, Second Edition

By

Dan and Dawn Williams

Introduction to (2nd Edition)

Living M/s was originally released in 2011 and although that doesn't seem like that long ago, when we reflect back on it - the iPhone 4 was just released, social media sites like Facebook were just starting to take off, and some new TV show called 'Game of Thrones' came out - we realize that a lot has changed.

A lot has happened for us since then as well. We decided to try our hand at running a hotel event and that resulted in the very successful Power eXchange Summit. Then, along with good friends Barak & Sheba, we followed that up by operating an alternative community space (The Columbus Space). When that was done, we sold everything and became full-time RV'ers, moving across the country and avoiding snow.

Throughout it all, as we presented around the nation or via our podcast, people continue to this day to reach out and thank us for the book **Living M/s**. A week before writing what you are currently reading, someone reached out and said they were doing an 'unboxing' of Living M/s and asked if there would ever be a second edition. That idea has been on our project list for years but we decided now was the time. So we rented a hotel room for a weekend, broke out the notes and the coffee, and began work on what has become the version in your hands now.

As we write, edit, and tweak, we are reminded again that this continues to be the foundation of who we are. Although we don't currently use the titles Master and slave (more on that below), a power exchange couple is still who we are and the guiding principle in our lives.

'Wait', we can hear you thinking, 'you are not Master and slave anymore?!' It is only a matter of the label. We retired the terms Master and slave much like we once retired using Dom and sub. Our growth and expanding relationship dynamic moved us to change. We now use Belum and belet, terms that suit us better. Dan is the Leader in a full-time power exchange relationship; dawn is his follower in a full-time power exchange relationship. The labels are just labels.

About the Authors

From the original 2011 Edition

Dan and dawn have lived together in a total power exchange Master and slave relationship for over 10 years as of this writing. They are well-known national presenters on M/s relationships, they lead dozens of presentations and workshops each year. They are also honored to be the 2010 Great Lakes Region Master and slave titleholders, representing a 13-state region, on healthy power exchange relationships.

Along with presenting, Dan and dawn also record and air a weekly internet radio show (podcast) called Erotic Awakening. Erotic Awakening focuses on many M/s topics, along with other topics of interest. Their ever-growing listener base includes both those new to the lifestyle as well as the more experienced across the world.

In their mundane life, Dan is employed as an IT technician in a Fortune 100 company and dawn is a full-time student, housewife, and licensed, ordained interfaith clergy; ministering to the alternative community. Together, they live in Central Ohio with various furballs and the occasional grandchild underfoot.

About This Book and Our Writing Style

This book is a composition of our essays and writings. Certain sections will begin with "Dan says"; others begin with "dawn says". Some will begin with "We believe," while others will be conversational, denoting who is saying what (and to whom!). We did not do this to confuse our readers (promise!), but this book is indeed a joint effort by two individuals who are both husband and wife and Master and slave. Our writings reflect not only our joint view but also the individual perspectives of Dan as Master and dawn as slave, each from our own experiences. If you have heard us present or lead a workshop, or listened to our podcast, Erotic Awakening, you'll be reminded of that same style—we write like we speak in a natural way.

There's one thing you'll notice right off the bat, and you'll find it either odd, annoying or perfectly normal. We spell dawn's name with a lowercase "d," and Dan's with an uppercase "D." We also mix up our sentence case just a bit here and there—"Master" written with a capital "M," for example; "Master and slave" may be written as "M/s." If this seems strange or gives you a bit of a grammar migraine, we hope that you will allow us this leeway—it works in our life, and perhaps you'll see some value in it...or you'll just let it go!

Disclaimer

This book is our reflection as two people who have lived a successful power exchange relationship for over 11 years. It is not intended to be the only way, the one true path, or the Gospel of M/s. But what we represent here has worked for us in practice and continues to work for us. "Take what you need and leave the rest."

We strongly respect each individual's right to personal gender identification. Because male Master/ female slave reflects our personal perspective, we tend to use those gender pronouns. Mix and match as suits you; it works just the same regardless of gender!

As we discuss Master and slave, or Owner and property, in this book, we are always referring to CONSENSUAL power exchange. The terminology of domination and submission does not refer to coercion or weakness.

We do not suggest or condone non-consensual slavery in any form. We acknowledge that great harm was caused in the past by non-consensual slavery and that the modern-day problem of human slave trafficking is very real, resulting in great pain and anguish. This book is not about those situations.

Terminology in this book is a reflection of a consensual power exchange relationship style that is agreed upon by two or more consenting adults and that benefits all involved. Any attempt to compare what is described in this book to events of the past or illegal trade in human beings is incorrect and a misinterpretation.

Finally, we are not making any judgments when we use the term "vanilla" to describe relationships or lifestyles. "Vanilla" simply refers to the standard societal norm of behavior (we'll define it under "Terminology").

Acknowledgements

From the original 2011 Edition

We would like to acknowledge some of the people who helped us make it this far.

In the beginning were John and mel, Gina, and others; they were present when Mid Ohio Rose and Leather (MORAL) was created. Upon occasion, we all pissed each other off.

Lee and bes and Kat and other founders of Central Ohio Real D/s (CORDs); things did not always go smoothly, but it was a great start for us.

Carey, Owen, Jan, Steve and Diane, Gino, Richard, and the rest of the crew of National Leather Association—Columbus; they gave us an understanding of stability, while unaware they were teaching, that they helped us structure our foundation as a couple. Steve and Kelly, Eric and Enid, joe, Professor Bill, "smiley" Karen, and Trigger: names, names, and more names of those who were (are) our teachers.

In our later days, when we had our feet under us, a new breed of teachers came along, hundreds of you; we sit here and fondly recall the gentle conversations as well as the arguments—all great lessons.

Dave and Amanda; for teaching us it was OK to be sexy and sacred. Barak and Sheba; as much as you say you've seen us grow, we've seen your growth.

Jade and Luthian, Tristan and Colten, and all the other event coordinators: you took a chance by booking a fairly unknown couple, and then you became our friends. We feel we did a good job for you, and you keep inviting us back. Thank you!

Master Gallad and slave kelly; for convincing us to run for the Great Lakes Leather Alliance Master and slave title, and the rest of the GLLA crew who believed in us. JL and Jess; they've been there for us since the beginning, supporting us in any way they could, and answering our questions (even though some of those questions must have seemed silly). The rest of the Dayton BDSM and Sterling Shadow folks; you cheered us on.

Graydancer; for inspiring us to work on the podcast idea. Jay Wiseman, for the offhand compliment that meant a lot to us as "young" presenters. Lee Harrington, for a conversation that was more interesting than the two people next to us having sex.

And, of course, everyone connected with House Metta; our association with you continues to be of great benefit and joy. It is an honor to have a home with you. We look forward to supporting you as you've supported us, and as we've been supported by others over the last 11 years.

Dan says...

Additionally, I need to thank Jerry H., to whom I owe my life (and he isn't even kinky!; dawn says "That we know of.")

A special thanks to my slave, Carmen, who I can't help but feel is still unfinished. I wish things had gone a little differently.

Amber 410, who was really the reason we got re-involved in the local scene and who served us admirably. Although you did not become our unicorn, we love you.

Amanda and "Good" Sheri and Eric—are you mentoring me or am I mentoring you? Either way, I keep learning.

slave jem, who serves us still today and has taught us a great deal about service (and technology). We are quite "fond" of you.

Karen, my beloved significant other: my deep gratitude to you for putting up with me, sticking around and teaching me about love in a new way—and who is "not vanilla."

Finally, thank you to those thousands of people who attend our classes and listen to our podcast, and the hundreds who have said to us: "Hey, thank you; this really helped me."

dawn says...

For some of the same reasons, I would like to thank those Dan has thanked as well as my amazing sister Teresa: Though you don't always understand the lifestyle I have chosen, but it means a lot to me when you say you don't have to because you just want to see me happy. I'm blessed to have such a sister as you.

Additional Acknowledgements for This Edition

Today, we 'raise a toast' to those above who are no longer with us. It hasn't been that long since we wrote our original acknowledgments, but we've seen many of you move on from this life to whatever lies beyond. John, Lee, Carey, Owen, Trigger, Master Gallad, and JL. We keep you in our hearts.

Forward 2024

I only teach one class on Power Exchange. It is called _"Submission is a gift and you should be cherished as the delicate flower you are" and other bullshit I do not tolerate_. I find it occasionally funny when a run book (the list of classes at an event) runs out of space and prints it as '_Submission is a gift and you should be cherished as the delicate flower you are_,' as the people that show up...are expecting something different.

The class reflects how I see Power Exchange relationships and our PE culture in general. I am not 'old school' or God's forbid, Old Guard (will come back to that in a minute). I simply have a style and method that works for me. I believe punishment is part of a healthy M/s dynamic and I assume submissives and slaves want to be pushed and challenged or they would not be signing up for a relationship with me.

But that is just what I think. In the days of soft doms and AI that write power exchange contracts and virtual collars, I am behind the curve on the modern-day PE experience. And believe me, when I say I don't think I am _correct_ or _right,_ I mean it. If you want to believe that a group of Elders are out there and that emulating the Old Guard is the path, great. Or that Leader/follower or Authority Transfer or Gorean or Library/book is the only way, wonderful. We - humans - get trapped in the words and the images and the 'I want to make sure I do things the proper way'. The truth is - there isn't one. If there is anything I've learned, every time I see a PE situation and think 'That won't work', the people involved stay together for years and years and are damned happy.

To be blunt, why I would even be writing a forward to this book is...well, amusing to me. My failing in power exchange is I am satisfied with the way things are and stopped driving to the next level. I am coasting.

This is what I respect about Dan & dawn. They have reinvented how they practice power exchange - from Dom/sub, to Master/slave, to whatever the hells they use now - and still keep the core intact: "The follower takes care of the Leader. The Leader takes care of the relationship. Everyone grows. Everyone smiles".

Sometimes they get involved in multiple partner hierarchy groups; sometimes it includes a long-term relationship with a vanilla person; or it is 'sell everything and drive around the nation with just them and a dog'. But the core - that power exchange central-themed life - stays solid and adapts.

PS – I mentioned Old Guard and that I would come back to it. It is fun to believe that it existed at some point. But it exists no more than...well, than I do.

Master Hank

In a random coffee shop in Sycamore, IL

August, 2024

Forward

From the original 2011 Edition

All of us who are involved in BDSM in general — and in living in a Master/slave structure in particular — had to start somewhere. At one point, none of us knew anything. Some of us just started in and made it up as we went along; some of us sought advice from those already in a Master/slave relationship, some of us sought information from the Internet (if there even was an Internet when we started); some of us combed through books (yet even good books on BDSM and Master/slave relations are fairly recent).

Regardless of how we started out, only with time could the vast amount of good and bad information and advice that we had absorbed slowly age and be blended into serious useful knowledge that enabled us to live harmoniously with our partner.

For many of us, the Master/slave path started out feeling as though we had somehow been dropped into a foreign land without having been given much (if any) survival training. As we looked around, we discovered that the language – thought generally familiar — was slightly foreign. Some of the concepts upon which people were making decisions made only partial sense. Warnings hinted at by some of those who had lived in this foreign land for some time seemed unrelated to our past experiences. We got the idea that it might be nice to have some kind of guidebook for this place, but the store selling maps and guidebooks wasn't yet opened. For many, it was simply too difficult to learn the language and customs of this land and they turned back, concluding that it was safer on their egos and peace of mind to get back to the safer territory off their prior known world. These people looked back and wondered how anybody could really live in that land, the land of Masters and slaves. Nice to visit, but...

I have no real knowledge of the percent of adventurers who are able to stay in a Master/slave relationship over a long period, but I'd guess that the survivors are a small percentage of those that began the journey in the first place.

So, why do I relate this fanciful tale? I relate it so you can have some perspective when I say that the store selling the maps and guidebooks about living in the world of Masters and slaves is now open and this gem of a book goes a long way towards providing the insights and tools that those seeking that magical land will need to know in order to survive.

This is a very well thought-out book of personal insights that invites readers to look into themselves and their relationships and to learn from a Master/slave couple who has been annealed by their experiences to the point that they have reached the very most senior levels of our Master/slave community.

In my personal view – having read virtually every book written that relates to Master/slave relationships – that this is one of the major books on this topic and that it should be on everyone's "must read" list whether you are only thinking of starting to form a Master/slave relationship or have been in one for years. If it were possible to do so, I'd make this book required reading for anyone starting out in the BDSM and/or Master/slave life. It would save them a great deal of frustration and heartache.

Dan and dawn have done a masterful job of describing, discussing, and explaining complex and often controversial topics through well-grounded personal experiences. This book offers a great many topics/concepts to consider. At the risk of introducing a personal revelation, I found many, many pearls of wisdom in these pages that would have been of immeasurable help to me had this book been available ten years (as I was starting out), five years ago, or even earlier this year. Don't let anyone fool you – living in a Master/slave structure takes a huge amount of work and you'll never stop learning.

I like their writing style; it's folksy yet concise. I like the way Dan and dawn have succeeded in producing a realistic and coherent account of a complex story. I like the way that concepts are so clearly explained through the recounting of every-day actions and activities. Finally, I like the way that they have been able to communicate these important messages by basing them on the underlying assumptions and beliefs of our M/s community.

While there is no part of the book that I disliked, I particularly liked chapters/discussions about collaring, slave contracts, and mindfulness. What gems!

Good job. Kudos to both of you.

Robert J. Rubel, PhD (Dr Bob)

Author of "Master/slave Relations: Handbook of Theory and Practice"... and a few other books.

Table of Contents

Introduction

Dan says...

I am not a big fan of book introductions. They either tell you what you are going to hear (so let's just get to it!), or they go on and on about how they got started. So, let's make this brief, shall we?

It all began when I was four years old...

Well, not really, and we can skip those next many years until we reach the point where, for the last decade, I've been living in a power exchange relationship. That is where this book really starts because that is the beginning of the experience on which this book is based. Although I've done a fair amount of research and study (which you will hear more about later), this is not a book of theory but rather one of direct experience.

I am a Master (or Dom in some circles—we will play with words and terminology in just a moment) in a full-time power exchange relationship. I am leader of a Master/slave (M/s) House. I am responsible for submissives and slaves in my care. One of them, dawn, had been mine for 11 years as of the writing of this book. Others have been with me for various time periods (for various reasons).

Although I've come across many books that discuss how to have great play scenes (some involving limited-duration power exchange) and can refer to a number of other good Master/slave books, dawn and I felt the need to share some insights that we feel have not been expressed in print. Ours is a story of "boy meets girl, boy collars girl, boy makes girl a slave...and then they get married and fall in love." Our story continues in a sustainable relationship, with that as a base.

In a M/s relationship, marriage is optional—it is sometimes chosen, sometimes not. Actually, love is optional, too, although we will be talking about Master/slave relationships which have significant emotional involvement.

dawn says...

As Dan said, this book is based on our personal experience. Why share our experience? We feel it is valuable to those interested in starting a M/s relationship. When others hear us talk about how we went from vanilla relationships to a M/s relationship created with intent, they want to know how we did it. There are many obstacles to overcome when all you've known is one way of being in a relationship. Some of the main questions I'm asked as the slave are:

- How can you let someone have complete control over you?

- Do you get to contribute to the relationship, or is it all about him?

- How can you call yourself an empowered slave? Isn't that an oxymoron?

- How can you be both a Priestess and a slave?

- Your writing speaks to me. How can my spouse and I incorporate this relationship style into our lives?

We've been asked the same questions in person by many different people. I hope we can answer those questions here, once again, through our writings and reflections.

We don't have an exact formula to share or a list of specific steps to follow if you want to live a M/s relationship. We don't want to tell you how it should be done, because there isn't a single one-size-fits-all answer. What we can share with you, though, is how one couple did it: Dan and dawn, the only couple for whom we can speak.

Dan says

Thus, this book, a collection of our writings, thoughts, discussions, and essays, has been born. Beyond what we have promised above, it also includes thoughts on our changing terminology; the communities of M/s and BDSM and how they dance together (and apart); styles of D/s and M/s; M/s and polyamory; leather; orchestrating situations with multiple slaves; and other topics as well.

So, let's get started, shall we?

Let's Get Started

Speaking the Same Lingo

Dan says...

To see if we can come up with a common understanding, it is necessary to look at the words we use and how we mean them. Unfortunately, this is tricky. Webster's Dictionary is of little value to us (the definition of "submissive" used in Webster's is much different than "the person who looks good in a corset and collar going to formal dinners with me"). Although many lifestyle-friendly books and websites have covered terminology, often they do not agree with each other.

This can be a real issue for both new people and veterans alike. Written resources do not align with each other, and common usage (or misuse) is further mucking up definitions. In many areas and forums throughout the United States, the terms "bottom" and "submissive" now mean the same thing. Yet "submissive" is also (to many) a term that describes part of a power exchange relationship. Thus, a submissive in a power exchange relationship may feel that common usage has devalued the term "submissive."

I will freely admit my agreement that messy language helps no one, and I find it to be rather a shame. But then I take a breath, step back, and realize my opinion isn't really that important in the face of the fast-moving internet world. For some now, being a "Domme" is as simple as creating an avatar in a video world; claiming the title "Master" is no more significant than making it part of your profile on an alternative social media site. It feels like the language and value of these titles will continue to be devalued.

What to do about this? For me, my response is to continue to refer others to reliable sources ("I know that MasterDragonSlayer843 posted to the internet that the term golden shower is when you make money being a ProDomme, but perhaps you should check out some of these other resources..."). Live the words as you believe them. Create places in which language and its value— and, therefore, the value of words, titles, and labels—holds true; places like your M/s House, your Leather Family (which we will discuss soon), or your relationships. While it is tempting to try to change the world to your view, your energy may be better spent living your view, thereby teaching by example.

With all this in mind, we'll present some definitions of words and chat about their meaning, based on what we have learned from our experience in the real-time kink and sexual education world. Listen to us, and listen to others as well, then decide what makes sense for you

Terminology

Dan says

Some definitions we'll keep simple; just a sentence or two. Some, we'll explore in more depth.

- **BDSM**: This is a bit of a catch-all acronym with several meanings, including Bondage/Discipline, Dominance/

submission, and Sadism/masochism.

- **Top**: The person who is swinging the flogger, doing the fisting, tying you up, suspending you, or doing all those wonderful things to you. A Top can be a submissive, Dominant, switch—or none of the above.

- **Bottom**: The person receiving the flogging/fisting/bondage, etc. Again, this person can be a submissive, Dominant, switch—or none of the above.

- **Dom/me**: "Dom" is a male dominant; "Domme" is a female dominant. Often people who introduce themselves as a Dom/me really mean they are a Top. Dom/ me is also used by the Dominant in a power exchange relationship. We'll talk more about the difference between Dom/sub and Master/slave later. Domme is also used by female professional Dominants who charge for their services as a Top.

• **Submissive**: As with Dom/me, a submissive can either be a bottom or be their role in a power exchange relationship. There is no male/female version of the word.

• **Master/Mistress**: The person leading a power exchange relationship. Although Master is used primarily by males, in some circles females may be called Master. We have an entire chapter devoted to what a Master is, so this is all we need to say about it now.

• **Slave**: The person in a power exchange relationship who is not in charge. The term is non-gender specific. A later chapter will explore the slave concept in depth.

• **TPE**: Total Power Exchange. A relationship in which one person is the leader and one is not. The exercise of a TPE relationship may be detailed in a contract, with well-defined roles.

• **Scene and Play**: A scene is a negotiated session of BDSM activity. Play is the actual activity itself. So, you and your boy talk about heading down to the basement, bending him over the ottoman, and spanking him until he cries (or cums). That is the outline of the scene; spanking is the play.

- **Safewords**: A pre-arranged signal during a scene, that a bottom can easily use to communicate if they need to slow down or stop the scene. "Red" is for "stop" and "yellow" is for "change something up". A top needs to respect these signals.

- **Negotiation**: The process taken before a scene or starting a M/s relationship. This is where discussion takes place on what each party wants or doesn't want. This is also where terminology is agreed upon and safewords are discussed.

- **Collar**: A piece of jewelry that represents a person's role in a relationship as a submissive or slave. Some use the terms "training collar" or "collar of consideration." Since we don't have experience with these types of collars, we'll not expand on that definition.

In our introduction to this section, we mentioned the issue of people in our community using words in different contexts. Here are our definitions of a few more words/concepts; they will help set the tone for the rest of the book:

- **Lifestyle**: M/s is more than just a playtime activity, and that's a theme that runs throughout this book. Perhaps you are already thinking, "I get it: M/s is not play." We'll continue saying this because we find there are a lot of folks who don't get it; they continue to use the terms "Master/slave" and "power exchange" for "scening." Don't get us wrong;

we certainly don't object to scening or playing. Dan certainly enjoys Topping, using either a flogger or being Dominant. But, as we've stated, BDSM activity is how we play; M/s is how we live. We live our ethics, and we take responsibility for the dynamics of our consensual power exchange relationship.

• **House**: A group of people who view M/s or D/s power exchanges and the ethics of M/s, in general, in the same way. They may or may not live together and may not even be in power exchange relationships with each other. Some call this a Leather family. When people share like views, ethics, and a similar "heart" regarding M/s, they often form a House or Leather family. In a later chapter on a M/s House, we'll break that concept out in greater depth and give you some examples related to our House. But for now, a "tribe of like-minded folk" will suffice. For example, when we use the word "mentor," referring to a peer-to-peer relationship, people in our House understand "mentor" to mean the same thing we do.

• **Mentor**: For us, being mentored when we began our journey as a M/s couple was (and continues to be) very important. Being able to learn from others who have lived the life that we desired to create, walking the walk, was invaluable. Later we'll discuss our specific beliefs about mentorship.

- **Vanilla**: This simply refers to something or someone not kinky, like a general social event or a person who does not participate in kink activity. This is not a bad thing, nor is it a term of scorn. It just is what it is. We don't play golf, so people call us non-golfers. It's not a judgment; it doesn't mean we're better or worse individuals than golfers; it simply means we don't golf.

- **Leather/Leathers**: Leather is another catchall term used to describe our community or our tribe. Leather also refers to leather clothing, some of which can have traditional or deeper meanings.

What Does Living M/s Mean?

Golly, It's Just Like Real Life!

Dan says...

So, what does Living M/s mean? We'll have to explore the idea of M/s as a lifestyle for that to make sense. Although there are internet groups named "It's Not a Fucking Lifestyle" (yes, really), it is a lifestyle for some including, specifically, me and my House). As we have said, "BDSM is how we play; M/s is how we live."

M/s as a lifestyle means it is not something we turn on and off. It is how we live authentically. No, our slaves are not chained in our home all day long, waiting for the pleasure of some Master or Mistress. No, I can't demand service from someone not bound to me, be they M/s-identified or not. Further, it doesn't mean that I expect people who do identify as M/s to treat me as a "Master"— unless they choose to do so or, of course, if they are instructed to do so by their Master/Mistress.

M/s as a lifestyle is simply who I am (and in a relationship, who dawn and I are) all the time. I am always responsible for my slave, regardless of whether I am at work, at home, or at a PTA meeting. I am a Master, no matter the circumstances at any given moment. However, I only require those bound to me to view me in that light, not the entire world! So, at work I'm not acting as a Master; I'm simply Dan. I don't wear my leathers; I don't demand time off to attend BDSM or M/s conferences (although that's usually how I use my vacation time!). I didn't make small talk about us running for or winning the Great

Lakes Master and slave title. My slave is not chained to anything—which is a good thing because she has too much to do!

When we were both gainfully employed, we shared the housework. I handled the cat litter, dawn did the grocery shopping, and we took turns cooking. When I was unemployed, I increased my share of the housework accordingly. As of this writing, dawn is unemployed and does all the housework. Not every M/s couple structures their lives this way, but this way is our choice. Our first preference would be for me to work and dawn to stay home cooking, cleaning, and tending to my whims. But because I like having the economic freedom that comes from both of us having paid employment, I choose that dawn work outside the home. When she is not employed, though, there is no question as to who has responsibility for the housework. And if things change such that I am no longer employed, then I will put on an apron and do my share; you can call me "Mr. Mom" (or Master Mom, as the case may be!). This division of household labor has nothing to do with us having a valid power exchange relationship; it has everything to do with us having a thriving relationship. But, to be honest, housework chores are but one aspect of dawn's duties—she is also involved in taking care of the long, ever-expanding list of things we do, like scheduling our time, booking events, packing, taming our crazy calendar. My slave tends to, and is good at, these duties. She can be coy, or she can bite (in a kind fashion) as need be.

You may be thinking: "This is just normal relationship stuff, right?" Well, normal, healthy relationship stuff. This is the background. This is the foundation upon which we build our power exchange, a relationship of mutual respect. We understand that, although we may prefer that I didn't have to work and could laze around while my slave pampers me and feeds me grapes, and the cat uses the toilet and flushes after himself, thank-you-very-much, our real world is not like that. And living M/s requires that we live in the real world, with our M/s lifestyle defining how we live in that world, as part of that world.

M/s relationships come in a variety of types and flavors. And although an Owner/object relationship works for some, Owner/property might be more your line. They sound the same, but they meet different needs. Master/slave and Dom/sub are two sides of the same coin...or are they? As we explore, see what makes your heart light up and makes you feel at home.

Throughout this book we will look at both the pieces of the relationship—the Master, the slave—as well as the combinations and what can be created by those combinations.

Intensely Authentic: No Room to Hide

For me, a M/s relationship is much more intense than any other style of relationship that I've seen or been involved in. In M/s, there isn't any room to hide from yourself or your partner. Because it is so different, it requires you to look at yourself and your needs, and then make an informed decision whether or not M/s is how you want to live, knowing in advance that many will not understand you, and most won't support you. You have to either embrace your true self—or smother it.

For Dan and me, we each looked within ourselves, then sat down together to look at our needs, wants, and desires. We put them on paper, creating a contract and agreeing to abide by that co-created contract. How many other styles of relationships do this? We were both previously married, and neither of us can tell you what was in our marriage vows. We had no idea what we were trying to create within our marriages. We just knew we were doing "what people do." Whether it was because you're in love and taking the next expected step, she got pregnant, or grandma threw a fit when she discovered you were living together—getting married is what you did. And in this day and age, marriage is supposed to be a 50/50 partnership, whether or not it fits with your personality. Dan and I had both experienced something like that before; this time, we wanted something completely different. We knew what we wanted. After examining ourselves individually, we shared our secrets, and our most secret desires, with each other. Our relationship was built around being our authentic selves. Dan needed to be in charge and to be trusted completely, without reservation, by a strong person. I needed to completely trust someone: someone to whom I could surrender myself and my ego; someone who was strong enough to fearlessly show me his true self; someone who saw my submission as a gift and my slavehood as a strength; someone to whom I could give my complete support; someone who would support me in my healing path; and someone who would be my partner in all our endeavors. I must admit, too, that there was a thrill at the idea of being with someone who cared about me and was strong enough to control me; it was even very erotic.

Our relationship is built on trust. Yes, ALL relationships should be based on trust...but, unfortunately, my experience tells me differently. I've worked with groups of women in diverse environments, yet it always seems to be the same: when they talk about their relationships, they talk about how weak their men are, how they can't trust them, or how—as women—they feel they can get away with things. They seem to take pride in the fact that they have their husbands "pussy-whipped." They constantly tear their husbands down. They gloat over how they have saved their man's infractions in a mental file to use against him in a later argument. Many talked about how they hid money or lied about how they spent money. Everything seemed to be a challenge, like a chess game; a competition.

Many of the women with whom I worked or attended college would talk about how they couldn't share their fantasies or secrets with their spouses. Sometimes they would tell me, or hint at their sexual fantasies. When I responded that I imagined how exciting those fantasies must be to their spouse, they would look at me in shock, saying: "I can't share that with him; he wouldn't understand." I couldn't fathom being in that kind of relationship again. I just don't want to be in a place where I have to hide myself or keep secrets out of fear.

So, when Dan and I built our relationship, we tried to design it so that neither of us would ever have to live in fear of one of us finding something out about the other. I NEEDED to be in a relationship where my spouse knew everything about me and still loved me for being me. I NEEDED to be in a relationship where my spouse could share everything about himself without fear of my judgment.

What's Love Got to Do with It?

Dan says...

We've been asked "Can a M/s or D/s relationship exist without romantic love?" The answer is yes, and many do. But is it what you want?

Now, most of my M/s relationships have had emotional connections. I am deeply in love with dawn. But that is not the only way to live M/s.

I am reminded of a situation many years ago when I was still new, viewing all this "power exchange" stuff with fresh eyes. A Dominant offered a submissive friend a chance to live on a houseboat. The deal was that she would live in a cage, being let out to serve his needs. That situation was a complete and total negotiation. Her lot would have been that of a possession, nothing more—or less. After considering this opportunity for some time, she decided against it.

But the idea that she even entertained this—and explored the idea with some due diligence—was a shock at the time to many of us in our little M/s community. Didn't she want to be cherished, we wondered? Didn't she want to be a pet, to be loved, cared for, and about, exchanging her taking care of her Dom for, in turn, being taken care of by her Dom? She said no and that, as a matter of fact, she had broken off a past relationship because her Dom had fallen in love with her.

For her—and for others—M/s is not about a loving, committed relationship or a direct exchange dynamic in the way most of us would see it. It was about knowing her place, and her place as property. Some will argue whether this is healthy, or whether any sane persons would allow themselves to be used in such a one-sided manner. But is it one-sided? Or is the exchange just of a different sort?

We have already broken the bounds of "normal" relationships when we come to M/s. Some of us take a loving relationship and add a layer of power exchange to it. My slave and I took a power exchange relationship and added love to it (a small difference, you might say, but a significant one). Others simply seek the power exchange—the Master and slave dynamic—without an emotional aspect. The aspect they seek comes from within, born of service. They will also argue that love gets in the way of a "pure" power exchange. It gives the slave too much power whether she wants it or not, and the Master now has to battle his desire to love her or treat her as an object without bias. It can get difficult.

dawn says...

For me, today, my preference is to be in an M/s relationship in which love is part of the dynamic. I understand that love can temper some of the decisions, but without love involved, I don't know that I want a Master making decisions about my life. This style of relationship is also about growth. I want someone to care about me as a person; I want to know that, when he pushes me through my fears to do things I want to resist, he's doing it for my own good. He has no intent to harm me. Based on that knowledge, I can put aside my fears and walk forward.

Knowing Dan, I can see him lending me out to another Master for training purposes, to provide me with a new experience or two. At the top of the hierarchy, though, my Master will still be there. Because of that, and because I know that what he is doing is done out of love for me and our relationship, I will be able to do as he asks.

Playing Chess

dawn says...

Some ask me why, if I'm such a strong person, I would allow myself to be in a power exchange relationship. For me, the answer is simple: I don't like, nor am I good at, playing chess.

What does that mean? I don't like the power struggle. In my previous relationships, I was the standard vanilla wife or girlfriend. Everything was about who would "win" and who would make the decisions. Well, not everything, of course, but a lot of the time it certainly seemed to have that energy. What color sheets would we buy? Well, he wanted black and I wanted purple, for example. If he didn't allow me to get purple, he was pushing me into a decision that benefited him. If I changed my mind to black, I couldn't say anything because I'd be giving up my "position" on the chess board and he might see that as a "win" later to be used against me.

How we spent money: a chess move; what movie we saw: a chess move. I just didn't like it. And since it was about strategy, I couldn't believe the answer if I asked him what movie he preferred, because the response was usually: "It doesn't matter to me." Then, after the movie, he'd say: "You know I don't like that kind of movie. I can't believe you took me to see that. You should have known better." Then, all the friends would be told how it was my fault for taking him to a stupid movie. A price was paid, and a lesson was learned: not to trust what I was told.

Now, in case any former partner of mine reads this, I'm not necessarily writing about my relationship with any specific individual; this also covers my family of origin, my past boyfriends, a girlfriend or two, etc., etc.

Many, many individuals live in relationships where chess is the normal, everyday game. They either like it or maybe they don't know there are other options. I learned that I don't thrive in that atmosphere. It always felt like there was a hidden agenda that I just didn't get.

So, this time I chose a relationship in which it was agreed upon—upfront—that chess was not our game of choice. With us, there isn't really a competition; instead, we each get to help our partner. That's the game we play. If he asks me what movie I want to see, and I say it doesn't matter; that is truly what I mean. He trusts that I'm telling the truth. He doesn't have to second-guess me, and he knows that there won't be a price to pay for the decisions he makes.

If we go to buy sheets and he wants black and I want purple, I'm allowed to tell him why I want purple. He weighs the choices, considers my words—or not, and decides; OR he decides to leave the choice up to me. It depends on how important the sheet color is to him. There is no "win/lose." There is no strategy involved. There is no "Well, you got to choose the sheet color so I get to choose the rug color." One choice/decision does not affect any other.

Some will not understand this concept. When I try to explain it to those who don't get it, I get a blank stare. Or they think that I've been brainwashed or something. It's not that way at all.

I've looked within myself. I have found a piece of my authentic self.

This is the type of environment in which I thrive.

Broken Vase and a Junkie

Difference between Abuse and Power Exchange

dawn says...

I'm very open about being a survivor of childhood abuse.

People have a hard time understanding how a survivor of abuse, be it childhood or domestic, physical, mental, or emotional, can be involved in this lifestyle. Partners, friends, family, and maybe even the survivors themselves, have doubts as to how anyone with such a traumatic past can be involved in an M/s dynamic.

I did. I wondered how I could be interested in such a "violent" lifestyle when I had such an abusive past. Hell, so did my ex-husband and some of my closest friends at the time. They were worried about me when I finally admitted to myself that this is who I am and the lifestyle I need.

But I did not let that stop me. Once I opened the door to look at my authentic self, I figured out many things about both myself and the M/s lifestyle.

First of all, take the word "violent." I bet some of you sucked in your breath, ready to correct me when I used that word. Why? Because you've already figured out, like I have, that violence is NOT what this lifestyle is about. I enjoy BDSM but it isn't always a part of M/s.

Second, this has been the most healing path I've ever taken. I seriously believe that had I not found this path, along with such a trusting and honest partner, I would not be as far along as I am in my healing.

With that said, telling a little of my background may be in order here. Don't worry, I won't go into details.

I must admit to believing in "WooWoo" ["Woo" is generally used to refer to the spiritual path of BDSM, M/s, D/s]. I truly believe that the Universe showed me this path and the partner with whom I would be traveling the path. How else could I have known someone for so many years without having a romantic interest in him? What's the likelihood that both of us would find this path at the same time—and the same place? It happened, of all places, in a major bookstore. I had worked so hard my entire life to build my walls; they came crashing down during a non-consensual healing session. I call it non-consensual because I didn't consent to it being a healing session. The fact that it became the pivotal point in my healing was neither my fault nor hers. That's just how it turned out. This happened at a workshop that a woman was giving in the middle of a bookstore. It sounded interesting in the newspaper, so I went. Dan and I were the only ones to show up. He wasn't supposed to be there with me. He was supposed to be at a meeting, but the meeting was canceled, so he decided to tag along with me. The workshop was a type of divination using muscle responses of the person's body, called kinesiology.

As with any form of divination, I decided to test the practitioner's skill by asking her a question the answer to which

I thought I already knew. What did I ask her? I asked her why I couldn't lose weight. She took a breath, closed her eyes, and held my wrist. She started asking questions really fast. I couldn't make out the questions but felt her fingers flex around my wrist as she whispered. Somehow, my muscles had answered all her questions. Within about five minutes, she knew all my deep, dark secrets. She knew things that I had never told anyone. Slowly, she shared this information with me in a soft tone that no one else could hear. I thanked her, feeling my walls crumble, right there in the middle of the store. Dan had not heard our conversation; as I ran out the door, he chased after me.

I had a meltdown in the parking lot. He wasn't exactly sure what to do, so he let me talk. We talked for hours. Well, I talked. He listened and told me, over and over again: "It will be OK." I did something I had never done before: I shared everything with him. I gave him all my memories. He didn't judge me. For the first time, he held me. He saw the pictures of what happened to me as a child; pictures that, for years, I had been carrying around in my head. Mine is a story of sexual abuse and mental abuse, as well as emotional and physical abuse. In the past, I had tried to share these memories with others, but no one ever felt that they could handle it. The few times I tried, I was asked not to share. Dan was strong enough to listen, and then to let go. This was the beginning of our foundation of transparency and trust.

Many others have stories similar to mine. Some are less severe, some are more so. The details are not important. What happened to me and to others destroyed our ability to trust.

It destroyed our self-worth. We took it out on ourselves and on others around us. Some may have even forgotten what happened until they became adults and something triggered the memories. Some of us have spent years and years working with counselors and psychiatrists, with results ranging from great to not-so-great.

Dan and I found this lifestyle, and when people also found out about my abusive history, they put two and two together—and got a totally wrong answer. They thought they saw a correlation where there wasn't any. In their defense, though, I must say that at first I, too, wondered if there was a correlation. Why not? It's what psychologists and psychiatrists were being taught. But for me, I couldn't believe something that felt so good could be wrong.

I'm the type who has to get to the bottom of things, to get my questions answered. I began to ask questions. I asked individuals in BDSM groups if they were abuse survivors. I found out that, of the many people I questioned, the ratio was about 50/50. This was not the most scientific way of conducting research, not even close. But it gave me hope. I found that someone's abusive history was not the reason why they chose BDSM or M/s over a vanilla life. I know people who have an abusive past and are in the Leather lifestyle. I know others with abusive histories who are NOT in the Leather lifestyle. The same goes for people who had perfectly happy childhoods; some are here with us...some ended up vanilla. This tells me that, for most of us, abuse is NOT the determining factor as to which side of the fence you decide to play. I also found no correlation as to whether individuals ended up on the Topside or the bottom side. Of the abused individuals I know, there are just as many Tops as there are bottoms. It just depends on your wiring/make-up as to which side is of more interest to you.

Now, others believe that we survivors are trying to role-play our childhood. I have to disagree. There may be some who do this, but after many years, I still haven't run across any. How can I say this? Well, what are the three most well-known guidelines of BDSM? They are "Safe, Sane, and Consensual." Let's think about that for a moment. Safe, Sane, and Consensual. How can you be consensually abused? Abuse is about taking power from someone WITHOUT their consent. Therefore, in an abusive situation, the key missing ingredient is consent. Abuse is not safe; abuse is not sane; abuse is not consensual. So, reliving abuse consensually simply isn't the same animal.

In my situation, I had no choice. I had to deal with the hand that was dealt to me in my life. How is that consensual? How about sane? If it was sane or consensual, why was it done in the dark and kept secret from everyone? And safe? You won't find BDSM classes or workshops on how to dish out abuse safely and get away with it.

Do you know what drew me to BDSM and an M/s lifestyle? It was the idea of trusting someone completely; the idea of having so much faith in someone that I'd allow them to tie me up and to be completely in control of my body. I was a master at disassociation. Is that reliving abuse? You can't convince me of it no matter how hard you try. There is a completely different energy to what we do, compared to what was done to us.

Though I am a slave, I am a slave by choice. It's about getting to know yourself, your needs, and your wants...about how you want to live and with whom you want to live. Our lifestyle involves protocol, rules, and boundaries. I absolutely love that part.

One of the main guidelines of my spiritual path is: "As it harms NONE, do what you will." This means that, if it doesn't harm anyone—including YOU...have fun! And that's what we are doing. We are having fun. We aren't harming anyone. We are consenting adults, fulfilling fantasies in a healthy way. There is no way to compare our chosen, consensual lifestyle with our histories. They are completely separate.

Now, with that soapbox rant over, on to the next topic that affects survivors: triggers. Lucky us. As survivors, most of us will find our triggers. Triggers are things or events that remind us of those times when we had no control and did not consent; times when we were hurt; and times when we were harmfully degraded (obviously it was harmful if it still strongly affects us today). Some of us even suffer a more severe form of triggering, called Post-Traumatic Stress Disorder (PTSD). This is what military veterans suffer from after returning from the battlefield. Sights, sounds, smells, and movements: can cause flashbacks that send us back to hell. If we want to get the most enjoyment that we can from this, our chosen lifestyle, then we need to learn how to deal with our triggers. Our partners need to know about our triggers in order to safely play with us or command us. Dan has had to work through a lot of this with me. For example: I once asked him to take some naughty pictures of me. He spread me out on the bed, got out the camera, the flash went off...and I instantly curled into a fetal position. I was gone. Luckily, because Dan knew of my stories, he was aware that something like this might happen. He was able to bring me back by talking calmly to me, reminding me where I was and that he wouldn't hurt me. He had me take a deep breath, and another, until I came back. And then I cried. We worked on this trigger for a while. Little by little. It takes patience. But it's worth it. I didn't want this trigger to have control of me. I'm now an exhibitionist who loves to have her picture taken!

Now, I do have some triggers that I haven't been able to completely overcome. But, I can honestly say that, through the structure and freedom of a TPE relationship with a Master who understands and supports my road to recovery from the past, this relationship has been the healthiest relationship I've ever experienced. I am me. In this relationship, I can't hide my past; I can't keep secrets from him; I am unable NOT to be my authentic self. This relationship has been healing. This relationship gives me the strength to overcome having been a victim.

Being the Master of an Abuse Survivor

Dan says...

When we began looking into total power exchange as a lifestyle choice, it was important to us that we understood who else was seeking this lifestyle. We wanted to be certain that this could truly be a healthy choice. Some told us that the lifestyle was only chosen by those who were raised with some sort of abuse in their lives; codependent; naturally weak-willed; overbearing bullies; or simply those unable to otherwise find mates.

We did our research. Although abuse survivors are in the lifestyle, we found that there are about as many abuse survivors in the lifestyle as there are in any other cross-section of society. The assumption that abuse survivors gravitate to being submissive is no more correct than the assumption that abuse survivors would lean toward being dominant. In addition, there are just as many Masters and slaves, Dominants and submissives, and Tops and bottoms who don't have any kind of abusive past.

This knowledge is important to us because my slave, dawn, is indeed an abuse survivor, although I really dislike using such sanitary language to describe the many years of horrific abuse to which she was subjected by those who should have protected her. However, this book is not the place to vent my disgust at the way she (or any other human) was treated in the past. Instead, I want to speak about being the Master of an abuse survivor by providing some general reflections about how I deal with that aspect of my slave. Some things you will be able to apply directly; some will simply be an expression of my own background. I hope you find my reflections to be of value if sexual or other abuse is part of your slave's background.

For the sake of clarity, I am not speaking as a professional analyst, counselor, or psychologist. I am simply offering you my personal perspective, as well as that of others from whom and with whom we have learned during our journeys in the lifestyle.

Also, these words are intended for long-term, committed M/s relationships. If that does not apply to your relationship, then I suggest you tell your slave that there is some degree of limitation in this area. Don't try to "fix" your slave; offer guidance and encourage her/him to address the situation in an appropriate venue. This does not mean that an abuse survivor can't serve as your slave, or that you should push them away. Instead, be aware of your own limits. Know it is sometimes wise to say: "I don't know the answer or how to work through the process; please seek someone with the appropriate skill set." You might think that surprising your slave with a role-play scene from their past would be a great way to help them get over it; instead, that could be very dangerous because you might destroy trust and become associated with the abuse instead of the solution. Remember, too, that as the Master/Top/Dominant, if you create a scene that, unwittingly, triggers something bad in your partner, you can't just walk away and tell them to deal with it. You need to ensure they get the attention they need at the moment.

If you are in it together for the long term, then the first thing you need to do is give yourself permission to utter a very powerful phrase: "I don't know." Those words empower you, and they empower your slave. If you, yourself, are not an abuse survivor, you won't understand what your slave is going through. You may be tempted to tell her/him to just "let it go," "man up," or suck it up and keep on truckin'. Believe me, your slave would love nothing more than to just "let it go." However, in talking with people about abuse and its aftereffects, commonly known as post-traumatic stress disorder (PTSD), simply making a decision to let go is sometimes not enough— and "letting go" may not even be possible.

Now, since we have established that it is OK for you to say "I don't know," go do some studying. Look into PTSD to get an idea of what it is, what it means, and how it can affect individuals. You do not need to become an expert but do become at least knowledgeable enough to understand the long-term effects of PTSD. Do this for YOU, not for your slave. You need to understand that there will be situations, no matter how good a Master you are and how willing your slave is, when a "trigger" will pop up that may result in your total loss of control. It will be of great value to you to understand that the problem may not be either you or the slave; the slave's lack of compliance may be due to the past, the PTSD, or some other external cause. I spent many frustrating times wondering if I lacked the skill to communicate what I wanted or if dawn really wanted to obey. I eventually learned that at times the issue was something under the surface we did not know about...or were not ready to see.

If you are willing, I suggest you find out about the abuse in your slave's life. In detail. I asked my slave to become completely transparent to me. Every gory detail, every incident, every facet... bit by bit. And with each part she revealed, in fits and starts, I was able to take a deep breath and say: "That was a horrible thing to go through. Now, take my boots off." I did NOT do this to demonstrate my coldness or lack of concern for her history or feelings; I first acknowledged what my slave said and then reminded her: "You are still my slave." Verbalize this to your slave:

- You are still my slave.

- Your value to me has not changed.

- The fact that you had a hard go of it in life is not a reason to change anything between us.

- You are no longer that abused victim, that person you once were.

- You are my slave.

It was of great value to my slave to know that I really was OK with who she is today and that the abuse was not her fault, regardless of having been told, or telling herself, that she was to blame. It is common for abusers to emphasize that the person being abused is causing the abuse, is asking for it, and is OK with it. I started to help dawn see those concepts as the lies they are.

It's important to encourage your slave to take a more direct, professional approach, too. I believe it is valuable for my slave to address her past via standard therapeutic means. She has spoken to counselors, psychoanalysts, shamans, and clergy as she has journeyed through her past toward self-acceptance. My job as Master is not to say: "Go see this counselor"; rather, my job is to support her actions. A journey of self-healing must be directed by the self. You, as Master, are your slave's foundation, cheerleader, and source of strength—but you cannot heal your slave, or make your slave seek true healing. The abuse survivor must WANT to heal herself/himself. Just as it's unlikely for a drug addict to succeed at rehab if s/he is doing it "for" mom, spouse, brother, or job— nothing works until the individual is seeking help for himself/herself.

I am proud to say that being a positive part of dawn's life has helped her as she went from abuse victim to abuse survivor. Now, she counsels others in the M/s and power exchange lifestyles who have also come from abusive backgrounds. Although it is, and always will be, a part of her past, it is just that—part of who she was. She is not her past, nor is she controlled by it. She continues to blossom into an incredible human, empowered by life and the path that she has traveled. Together, we are a much stronger couple because we looked into the past and did the necessary work to make the past just another chapter of life.

Recovery in the Lifestyle

Dan says...

Most people are familiar with the group Alcoholics Anonymous, more commonly referred to as AA. As it happens, sometimes people who are recovering alcoholics are also pretty damned kinky! This has nothing to do with AA or with being a recovering alcoholic; it's just statistics. Some kinky people are recovering alcoholics/addicts, some are NASCAR fans, some are Goth, and some are chiropractors.

I happen to be one of those recovering alcoholics/addicts: On March 30, 1991, I had my last drink and drug, and I have been "clean and sober" since then. I was kinky while I was still drinking, but I wasn't involved in (or really, capable of) power exchange or M/s dynamic relationships. This makes lots of sense because as an active alcoholic and user of interesting controlled dangerous substances, I really only cared for myself.

As I got sober, I started to learn about being more selfless and more responsible. At some point, the idea of leading a power exchange relationship and being sober just came together. And it has helped both my recovery and my growth as a person.

There are some aspects of recovery life and M/s life that seem to conflict. For example, the idea of powerlessness and surrender to a power greater than oneself is a key AA philosophy—yet being a Master says I do have power and that the buck stops here!

Fortunately, for people who are either kinky or involved in power exchange relationships, there is a recognized group within AA just for us. Called Recovery in the Lifestyle (RitL), they hold 12-step meetings in the classic AA format, and they include topics that are open and welcoming to those who have alternative sexual expressions. You can find RitL meetings in Chicago, Florida, and other places in the United States. dawn and I often run RitL meetings at different events.

The challenges of being a recovering alcoholic and Master (or slave) can add some additional wiggles to your M/s—we are very grateful that we are not alone.

Different Styles

Different Styles of being Master and slave

dawn says...

Dan will discuss how slaves can be different in different situations (though some may not agree, this reflects our experience). How is this possible? It's possible because each Master/slave combination is different as it relates to the couple's energy, their individual needs/wants, and their styles. As a result, it's important to know, at your core, what kind of Master or slave you are.

You could be a Master who enjoys micro-managing a slave or one who prefers to order a specific outcome and allow the slave to figure out how to accomplish your objective. You could be strictly into sadism and discipline. You could be a Master who sits on a couch all day, expecting your slave to take complete care of you. You could be a sexual Master, interested only in bringing out your slave's slutty side. It's imperative to know if any of your desires or behaviors are "hard-wired" within you because you'll need to find a slave who is similarly hard-wired.

Now, some of these things could change within the dynamic of each different relationship or even over the years within one relationship. For example, Dan is not, as of this writing, into micro-

managing, nor has he been over the past 11 years. While this has not changed over the years, it certainly could. Not micro-managing may be a core piece of Dan, something that is not going to change. Yet administering discipline versus helping his slave(s) to embrace their slut side could be something that changes; over time, this is something that actually has changed for us. As part of our individual growth processes, the focus of our relationship has changed from year to year. The focus has also changed to reflect the dynamic between Dan and his other submissives/slaves. In each case, it depended on what they were trying to accomplish together, as well as what he was trying, at the time, to teach them.

Though I like to take care of Master, he is not the type to sit on the couch and have me do everything. This is a good thing because I need a Master who is social and who creates something with his life. I need a Master who has a purpose because purpose is one of my driving forces. As we've said, whether Master or slave, you must each know who you are at your core. You could be a slave who wants to be locked in a cage all day, or one who wants to do domestic service. Maybe you want to be micro-managed. There are many options possible; describing who you are and what you need as a slave will tell you what you need in a Master.

Why is this important? Because if you need to be micro-managed and your Master doesn't like to micro-manage, neither of your needs will be met and, at some point, there will be conflict. If the slave is bi-sexual and poly, but the Master is monogamous and requires the same from the slave, it's best to know upfront. You may not be able to set your needs aside for very long. Some things that are hard-wired are going to arise, whether or not you want them to surface. Maybe as a slave, you need to be social, but your Master is a hermit and requires you to stay at home to serve him. You really have to know yourself and what you are looking for. If your styles don't match and your needs don't match, there isn't much hope for your relationship to be authentic—or to last. In the end, one of you will be ignoring your needs, and resentment will arise.

Now, it doesn't have to be all doom and gloom. There may be ways to get creative with this. Our relationships are alternatives to begin with, so we can create anything we want. For example, maybe as a slave, I need to serve a certain way that doesn't do anything for Master. He may decide to meet my need by loaning me out to another Master. Or Master may want to be served in a way that doesn't work for me, so he finds someone else to meet that need. I can't think of any service that doesn't work for me, so let's use the example of me having a hard limit of touching shoes. Because of that hard limit, he brings in another slave to do shoe service, such as bootblacking (polishing his

boots or shoes). Yes, I know. I said "slave" and "hard limit" in the same sentence. Again, different beliefs and/or structures work for different people. My Master allows me to have hard limits (I only have three, and touching shoes is not one of them!); we respect each other's needs—and limits.

So: know who you are, as well as what you need and what you simply want. Without this knowledge, you'll be in for a lot of heartache.

Different Types of Slaves

Some people who identify as slaves do not seek to give up total control of their entire life to another. They may target and focus on surrendering certain areas in their life. They may release their power over those areas while retaining a specific focus of their power. Conversely, they may have a Master who is only interested in one facet of keeping a slave, with their focus on accepting the gift of submission.

This should not be viewed as a weakness of any sort. It is a reflection of self-knowledge, of knowing what you want or need, or it may be an expression of desire. A slave may need to be possessed in certain aspects of his/her life, such as sexually or as part of a relationship yet need their freedom for self-determination in, for example, financial or family issues. Often, I've met slaves who desire to be controlled in a power exchange relationship but do not want that power exchange to impact their careers or how they raise their children.

A Master may desire a slave to keep his/her home clean and ensure the refrigerator is always stocked and may not want to influence the slave's education. Does that mean the Master is just a "player," one not worthy of the title "Master" because s/he isn't willing to wield full control?

In most cases, no. For example, at the time of this writing, I have a wonderful slave I've named jem; she assists in serving on certain nights, travels to some events with us, and also does some geek stuff for me. At the same time, she is preparing to graduate college and begin her career as a graphic designer. What level of influence do I exert in this? What level of influence do I want to exert? In this case, I want to exert little influence. My desire was to train a slave and build her a foundation as she moved forward with her life. She knows, as do I, that her destiny is to accept my training and then move on. I will not allow her to do anything that will harm her, but I also believe that in her position (she's young, strong, and smart), she has the world by the balls—and she should give those balls a squeeze. As long as she acts in an ethical manner, this is a great time to explore the world and herself so she can see what life has to offer her.

Creating and Documenting Your OWN M/s

43

Writing a Contract

dawn says...

Since Dan and I frequently talk about our contract, we have been asked to explain what a contract means to us and how can it be used as a tool in a M/s relationship. Here we'll share what worked for us. We understand that some people do not believe in having a contract for their M/s relationship. For them, a contract isn't needed because it's about someone being in charge and someone always following directions. We've heard of Masters who say: "The contract is that she is bound to me; she will, without question, do anything and everything I tell her to do." That may work for some.

Dan and I view our relationship as an expression of our core selves AND also as a tool for growth. Since we came from a background of vanilla relationships that didn't work for us, with no experience in power exchange, we wanted to define what it was that we were looking for, wanting, and needing in our relationship. With that in mind, we formed our contract.

So, what is an M/s contract? To begin with, it's NOT a legal document—nor should that be its intent. It is simply an agreement, written between multiple parties, used to clearly set forth and solidify their understanding of what they are co-creating as a couple living a Master/slave dynamic. It is an unambiguous statement of intent, goals, expectations, wants, and needs.

For us, there were more pros than cons to having a contract. We saw this document as a way of being proactive in our relationship, rather than reactive. We acknowledged that we are human and we make mistakes, so we agreed—ahead of time—to define in a document how we planned to handle those mistakes. This contract became the ultimate communication tool for us because it was written during a time when we were clear-headed; therefore, we knew we could refer to it later if things got rocky. It was also great at preventing any feelings of co-dependency. We could see, in writing, the healthy manner in which we had chosen to live. It also helped us express thoughts, feelings, and assumptions we each had but had not previously expressed until we wrote our contract. Dan and I put a lot of work into that contract.

There were some in our BDSM community who didn't understand why we needed this document. People expressed opinions that the contract was giving me too much power in the relationship and that a M/s contract should be nothing more than "I am His; that is the sum of our contract." Others told us that we'd outgrow the contract because contracts are stagnant. We took all this advice into consideration, and then we decided that, for us, the process of building a contract was a very important step for our relationship. We each had to dig deep into our own psyche to learn about ourselves and what we wanted, as individuals and together as a couple, before we could move forward.

Coming from a vanilla background, there were a lot of things that we had to unlearn in order to be able to embrace what we wanted. It's easy to fall back on vanilla because that's the predominant style of relationships around us. We can't go to our uncle and say "What do you do when Auntie defies your instructions about how to scrub the floor?" But, in our case, we have a written document in which we have agreed that if orders are defied, exactly how that defiance will be handled. For me, this document, and my knowledge that Dan would abide by his written word, gave me a sense of trust and security.

You will come to understand that, even though many think a slave is dependent and a Master is independent, in reality, an M/s couple becomes interdependent, relying on each other to balance each one's strengths and weaknesses. Submission can't happen without Dominance, and Dominance can't happen without submission.

Something to keep in mind is that healthy relationships change, adjust, and grow of their own accord. Therefore, a M/s contract isn't created as a stagnant document. Dan and I decided to review our contract every month, or at least portions of it, and, if necessary, to totally revamp it once a year. We usually do this review right before the anniversary of our collaring. The main pieces of the contract remain in place, but sometimes we change the focal point of our growth for the year. During our first year, we focused on our development in a M/s relationship. Year two was about learning and embracing high protocol. In year three we worked on finding our inner sluts, and so on.

When creating a contract, let it reflect the circumstances of the couple. Is it a live-in relationship or a long-distance one? Is it a training association or a loving relationship? Does it include financial aspects or the slave's schooling? Does it include sex? Does it include interactions with others?

Our contract covers everything because we are a married 24/7 couple in a thriving, growing, M/s relationship. Dan has had other slaves. One slave was for training only; there was no sex, and Dan had no responsibility for her financial state or schooling. Another slave had a husband and lived a few hours away, so her contract only covered certain aspects of her life. Each slave was different, and each contract pertained specifically to the expectations of each individual. For each slave, other than me, a time limit was built into the contract. That time limit may be extended beyond the original time frame, but each contract began with a time limitation. Although that restriction may change in the future with any other slaves Dan may bring in, that has not been our experience to date.

When building a contract, there are some things to keep in mind. First, approach it with honesty and integrity. Each party has the same responsibility to be vocal about their own needs and wants. Do not assume the other party will know your true desires, or that you both have the same definitions for the words you are choosing.

We also recommend building into the contract an exit clause, as well as the steps for the dissolution of the relationship. We were given this advice by a long-time member of our local Leather community. She had been writing contracts with her relationships for years and, although we trusted her experience on this issue, we really didn't want to include this clause. We were wearing rose-colored glasses and still flying high on NRE ("new relationship energy"), so we felt it would never be needed. However, we did find it to be important in our contract, as well as with other contracts over the years. We now consider the exit clause and dissolution plan to be healthy parts of a contract because if the relationship doesn't work, you know what steps you will take in order to part with honor and dignity.

There are some basic parts to a contract that we recommend you consider. Which parts you include depends on what you want out of the contract, as well as the relationship itself.

- Statement of intent: This begins the contract by stating who the involved parties are, on what date the contract will be activated, a general summary of what the contract covers, and the intent or goal of the contract.
- Terms: This section sets forth the style of the contract, such as whether it is a long-distance relationship, a sex-slave contract, a service contract, or some other type of contracted relationship. It also covers how often the contract will be reviewed and updated, as well as who can update it.
- Needs and wants: This can be the most difficult part of writing the contract. It takes complete self-honesty, as well as faith that the other person is being honest as well. We worked on this part for months. Dan wrote his section before showing it to dawn, and dawn wrote hers before showing it to Dan. Then we compared our

list. Believe us: this was scarier than any other part of the process. We knew that if any of our major needs didn't match, we would have to decide if we could make the relationship work. So we took our time and looked deep within ourselves. We made sure this list reflected what we needed and wanted for ourselves, not what we thought the other person wanted to hear.

- Duties: In this section, duties, expectations, and protocols are spelled out. It can outline everything from the slave's duties (like making the bed each morning) and behavior in public or when around others in the M/s lifestyle, to the Master's duties (like punishment of the slave).

- Rights: In the end, a M/s relationship is a consensual relationship. In this section, each person's rights are discussed. In our case, it covers how we will communicate with each other, as well as how we'll deal with emotional issues. We are partners in a relationship that has M/s as its foundation.

- Dissolution: This part of the contract is hard to write, and it is very powerful. Here you outline how the relationship will end—if it comes to that. For us, if something causes irreconcilable differences, we have created a list of steps that must be taken before either of us can be released from our relationship. We understand from past relationships that emotions can arise, and we both feel that this relationship is much too important to allow the heat of a moment to cause one of us to walk away in a huff. Our first step is to send an e-mail of intent; next, we've already chosen a mediator who will work with us. If nothing solves the problem and we both seek the end of the relationship, we will have a ritual during which, together, we will tear up our contract and burn it. We designed that ritual as the intense ending of an intense relationship, something not to be taken, or done, lightly.

- Exit clause: This is the "deal-breaker" clause: a list of things that instantly end the relationship. For us, there are two deal-breakers that would invoke the exit clause: drug use or cheating. Dan is a recovering addict, so if either of us uses drugs, it would be an automatic deal-breaker. Of course, if Dan used, I would want to take care of him and try to get him to help, but we both know what he's like when he's using, so I know the only way to protect myself would be to leave. This would be his final requirement of me as my Master. About cheating, what can we say? We are both poly and are in an open sort of relationship. We designed our contract with that aspect of our relationship in mind. Dan discusses his potential relationships with me, and as my Master, Dan has veto power over my relationships. Dan would, however, only exercise that veto to protect me, which he considers his responsibility. If I want to date someone else, all I have to do is to ask his permission. Because we have agreed that cheating is unacceptable, and we've agreed to total transparency, we know that cheating is a guarantee that we are destroying our relationship. Therefore, cheating voids our contract.

dawn says...

Whew! After doing all this work, have a celebration! Dan and I celebrated the original signing, and every year we celebrate our re-signing anniversary. After updating the contract, if necessary, to reflect our current needs, we invite our friends to a party, have a "testing" (more on that later), re-sign our contract, and then celebrate.

Sample Contract

The following contract example was written by a M/s couple who do not live together. It is a 24/7 relationship since the slave is always a slave to the Master and the Master is always Master to the slave. There are, however, limits within the relationship, and these are outlined in the contract. Our (Dan and dawn's) contract, however, is different in that it is much longer, about 8 pages with no time limit involved. It covers more because it is a design, a foundation, for a lifelong commitment.

(Editors Note: Dan and dawn's full contract can be found in the book Hearts & Collars)

Statement of Intent

This contract between the Master and the submissive/slave is intended to formally recognize the desire of the slave to serve the Master.

Terms

The slave seeks to enter the service of the Master primarily as a service slave and, as such will be trained in that style, as the Master sees fit.

The contract begins on September 12, 20xx, and will be reviewed on March 12, 20xx, with a potential extension for an additional six months, to September 12th, 20xx.

Duties

The duties, roles, and responsibilities of the slave will continue to be directed by the Master during the term of this contract. It is the responsibility of the slave to record and keep track of these roles. The slave will be responsible for keeping an active list of the commands that have been issued to her, and she must be able to produce that list at any time. The format of that list is up to the slave. Current duties include:

- Contacting the Master twice daily: first thing in the morning and again in the evening, to review the day's activities as well as her understanding of any responsibility given the previous day.
- Seeking permission before attending any lifestyle function.
- Seeking permission before engaging in play (BDSM scene, cyber, etc.).
- Seeking permission before dating.
- Being always on time, for everything.
- Seeking permission before taking on any responsibilities relating to any lifestyle group.

Rights

- Porch Time—The slave has the right to request Porch Time, a space of communication free of the protocols of a Master/slave relationship. This is to be used sparingly and only after other communication methods have failed.

Expectations

- Honesty—The slave will learn to practice complete honesty with the Master. This is essential to growth.
- Commitment—Prior to signing this contract, the slave and the Master have both agreed and accepted that they are making a commitment to which they will adhere until the expiration date.
- Relationships—Any relationship in which the slave may engage (romantic, scene, or power exchange) is at the whim of the Master. He may or may not allow such relationships, based on his perception of the slave's need for growth.

Play

- BDSM and Sex will occur during this relationship. The Master desires to assist the slave in an exploration of those areas of play in which she is interested.

Correction

- The slave understands that the Master will discipline her and punish her physically, as well as using denial, tasks, or other means.

Polyamory

- The Master, as of the date of this contract, is (and may continue to be) engaged in multiple loving and M/s relationships. The slave will respect those relationships, understanding that our Master/slave relationship does not occur in a void. It is essential that the slave have, or develop, an attitude of "and" rather than "or." Envy is an emotion to be addressed, cherished, and then released. Jealousy is an indicator that deeper issues need to be addressed; the emotion of jealousy, however, is neither bad nor good.

Limits

- Hard Limits—The Master and the slave agree the following activities will not occur between them, nor will they be explored during the term of this contract: latex (due to the slave's allergies); scat or golden showers; burning or cutting; blood play; cutting the slave's hair; and intercourse.
- Soft Limits—In time, these will be explored and pushed, with the Master's guidance, due caution, and diligence: N/A

Exclusions

- The following aspects of the slave's life are beyond the scope of this contract and, therefore, are out of bounds. Although the subjects may come up, the Master will not give any commands or orders relating to the slave's: finances; scholastic pursuits; diet; or family.

Dissolution

At the will of the Master, this contract may be declared null and void if the slave demonstrates a lack of integrity, lack of respect, or lack of growth.

This contract will be immediately void if the Master engages in any recreational drug use.

Signed by the Master and the slave this 12th day of September, 20xx.

Porch Time

dawn says...

One of the communication tools that we have written in our contract is "Porch Time." This is going to be a hard concept for some M/s couples to grasp and I can understand that. To us, Porch Time is a neutral space where we can express ourselves without our hierarchical roles and where we won't be punished for what we say or even how we express ourselves.

M/s works on many levels, but sometimes it may feel like the dynamic can hinder our ability to communicate in a productive manner. For me, it got to where I felt disrespectful if I spoke up about something minor that was bothering me or confusing me. Dan felt he didn't want to be judged over feeling foot stompy about something. Neither of us wanted to be judged, we are human beings after all, and needed to know that if our other communication methods didn't work, we had a 'free space' to fall back on. Over time, we've found that we don't often need this neutral space; however, if one of us needs it, we know it's there. We've also agreed that if Porch Time is called by either of us, it's super important and will be granted immediately.

So how did Porch Time come to be? Well, Dan felt it was essential that as a Master he foster a non-judgmental environment in which I could express myself. We created this free space before the contract was signed, but it seemed important to keep that space available. Journaling was used for a while, but he also felt it imperative for us to be able to communicate verbally in a neutral space. I had come from a past where I wasn't allowed to speak up. Dan wanted to ensure that I didn't feel "unheard," not only as a slave but as a human. By having this space where each of us could freely speak, more trust was created in our relationship.

We needed to form a neutral, physical space. This can be harder than it sounds. When we started, we had a two-bedroom apartment, two kids, and a cat. As you can imagine, there was no place to have discussions that weren't within earshot of the kids. So we would tell the kids that they couldn't come outside unless they knocked first, and we would go out onto the porch and settle in for talk time. The kids learned to respect this space, and they even called Porch Time themselves a few times over the years, having learned it was a space to speak honestly and openly, without fear of judgment or reprisal.

During Porch Time, we could set aside the formality of our roles as Master and slave; we could bitch, whine, and complain if we wanted. I could call Dan every name in the book (and make up a few new ones, if needed!), and it couldn't be held against me later. Dan could huff and puff at me, and I couldn't hold it against him as Master. We were a husband and wife trying to hash something out. Or we were whatever role we needed to be at the time that was not Master and slave. If I needed to call Dan on something (maybe it had to do with his addiction) and had to do it louder or more aggressively than

I was normally comfortable with doing.....I had the space of Porch Time.

Porch Time can also be a place of security for the slave if she is afraid of losing her voice in the relationship. We are human after all.

Now, since we incorporated this idea into our lifestyle in 1999, have we had yelling matches on the porch? Yes: once, maybe twice, over more than a decade and neither occasion had anything to do with our M/s dynamic. The subjects were ones that we had first tried to deal with in some other manner.

So, if we have this space that we've built where we can yell and bitch, why don't we do it more often? Because, no matter what, deep down inside we are still Master and slave. We still respect each other. We still have no interest in harming the other with our actions or words. We take Porch Time thinking that it's necessary, and then we end up talking with honesty and transparency—which is what we require in our relationship under all circumstances.

We still like the idea of a couple having a space, whatever they choose to call it, where they are able to bring up stuff for which they can't later be punished. Whether it's needed or not, remains to be seen.

M/s Ethics

Dan says...

A lot of people will tell you that M/s is an ethical lifestyle; and that honor, respect, integrity, and responsibility are part of our day-to-day lives. I believe that this is true—for many of us. It also has to be said that any group—be it an alternative lifestyle, political, religious, or model plane enthusiast—will include people who are involved for personal gain, for less-than-honest reasons, or for unethical purposes. There will be some assholes, too. So, I can make no sweeping statement that all M/s people adhere to high ethics. We have misguided people in the M/s lifestyle, and we have assholes.

The above caveat aside, I will say that the foundation of ethics in our M/s relationships provides the foundation from which those relationships can grow in a healthy manner. The strongest power exchange relationships are the ones with the strongest ethical understanding of both concepts and actions. These are two separate things and it is very important to understand ethical understanding and ethical action. As we discuss M/s ethics, we must first understand what they can be and then implement them; making 'ethics' a verb.

Ethical behavior can be your foundation in a storm. Additionally, awareness and practice of ethical behavior cause an internal and external shift. A focus on ethical behavior—such as refraining from gossip, acting in a trustworthy manner at all times, being honest when you screw up, and being responsible—causes an internal process that ensures you are worthy of trust and provides a deep self-assurance that you know who you are and that you are OK with who you are.

Further, do you want a Master or slave you can't trust? One who steals from their workplace? One who hides parts of themselves they don't want to admit exist within them? One who fears people knowing who they really are?

We will not turn this writing into a general book about ethics. We will, however, provide below the core principles of our house, House Metta.

- Respect—for yourself, for those in service to you and in relationships with you, and for the life you have chosen

- Honor—be true to yourself and to your ethics. Do not allow the terminology of M/s to imply that you can treat others with less honor than all humans deserve

- Growth—Take the hard path. Push, reach, strive, and grow. Always face forward and walk with courage toward your desire.

Mmm Sex

Dan says...

Recently, we were asked: "Is sex a big part of an M/s relationship, or just a little part?" The answer is actually neither of the above. Sex is an optional part.

I am a very sensual person and enjoy naughty bits as much as the next guy. For that matter, my slave dawn and I have done a fair amount of exploring kinky sex and such; some of our most well-received presentations are based on our slut play. We focus on using sluttiness as a form of expression and as a path of self-authentication, as well as self-deprogramming around what it means if you like really naughty kinky sex. (What does it mean? It simply means you enjoy really naughty kinky sex; this does not define who you are as a person, nor does it make you bad or unworthy of love, marriage, and/or happiness).

I've owned a number of slaves, and sex hasn't always been a part of those relationships. My most recent property is an average male's wet dream—but her training had nothing to do with my dick, and my dick had nothing to teach her. Further, what I wanted her to learn as a slave was actually made more powerful by not having that physical connection.

(On a side note: in my opinion, for male-bodied people, truly powerful leaders can fuck—or not fuck. But they do not make that decision based on what their dick feels is a good idea. Their dick's feelings might be part of it—but a powerful male can, regardless of biological urges, either have sex or not have sex. I'll not speak

for females on this issue because in my home culture, the United States of America, we totally screw up females by on the one hand telling them they are unworthy and bad if they enjoy sex...and then, on the other hand, we spend millions on advertising to convince women that they need to look even more sexy and that the advertised product will fulfill that need.)

dawn says...

Yes!!! Absolutely!!!

Well, the topic is sex, right?

I was somewhat confused when asked this question: "Is sex important to your M/s relationship?"

At first, I wasn't really sure what the person was asking.

I must say that originally the idea of being dominated sexually was a major turn-on for me, and it still is to this day. But, no, I don't need sex in my M/s relationship. To me, the power exchange itself is more important. I am His to command whether we have sex in our relationship or not.

Plus, both Dan and I are getting older. We have to keep in mind that there may come a day, at some point in time, when neither of us is very interested in sex. I don't really want to believe that, but I know it's a definite possibility. And if that day comes, it is OK. Our foundation is built on an ethical Total Power Exchange philosophy; because of that foundation, we will survive together even if the desire for sex and/or BDSM play disappears.

With that aside, my answer to the question is that the sex was and is still a major part of my fantasy world. I first learned of dominance and submission by reading paperbacks, then moved on to finding porn and stories on the early Internet bulletin boards (each one was known as a BBS). I found pictures and videos that involved people having their hair pulled, being commanded to do something humiliating or slutty, being spanked, or being slutted out to others. But I figured this was all fantasy, that no one really did this stuff or lived this way.

I started to collect pictures, videos, and stories; I couldn't get enough. I found people who really lived this life, and I began to believe in this as a possible way to live. Then, I started really looking at what it was about the pictures and stories that turned me on. I discovered it was the idea of being dominated and made to do the slutty things that I only dreamed about doing. I wanted to be the girl tied to the table and given to a group of men by her Master. That idea did it for me then and still does it for me now.

But I have found that scenario only works for me in reality when Dan, my Master, is involved. It is the Mastery and the power exchange that do it for me, not the sex itself, not the sluttiness itself.

I know this because I've gone alone to a swing club (with Master's permission, of course), where I could have been as slutty as I wanted to be. But it didn't work for me. Master wasn't there to command that I do something (or not do something, as His choice might be). The bottom line was my total lack of interest in having sex that evening. I realized that it wasn't about being commanded to do something that was sexual, it was about being commanded by my Master. The dynamic we have built, the trust He has earned, the power I have given to Him: those are the elements that make the sex with us so great. It is submitting to His desire that does it for me, whether that desire is for me to be with him or with someone else.

I have submitted to others in sexual and BDSM play but, again, it only works if Dan is part of the arrangement because I am, in essence, still submitting to Him. Those who understand TPE will understand what I'm trying to convey. My link, my bond, my connection is with my Master.

I make a terrible bottom. If I'm asked what my fetish is, I have to answer that I like being spanked, caned, and a variety of other things...but only if submission is involved. The toys and the play do nothing for me. I need to submit to Sir, even if it's through someone else, or the play is pointless for me.

Because of this, I know that we don't need sex in our relationship. Now, the sex is great! The play is fabulous! It is intense, explosive, and absolutely amazing between us. I'm not saying it wouldn't be hard to give up sex. But, for our M/s relationship to work sex is not a need.

Being a Master

Let's Get to Work: The Qualities of a Master

Dan says...

What makes you or me a Master? Many things are a part of being a Master:

- the responsibility for the slave and the relationship;

- the commitment;

- the guidance and education of the slave;

- the assistance in the slave's growth;

- the ability to demand performance; and

- the willingness to provide appropriate redirection.

It is never about being a dick, but it can be about being harsh. Yes, it is about being served by the slave, but it is also about fulfilling multiple responsibilities.

This section is part of the reason I am a big fan of contracts, at least at the beginning of an M/s relationship. When we are clear in our commitment to principles and our desire to push and be pushed, that's a good time to sit down and plan what we want the relationship to look like. In my first M/s relationship, we did exactly that. Although we have already discussed contracts, the point I want to make here is that for a variety of reasons it can be difficult, especially within a loving M/s relationship, for a Master to discipline or punish his slave. I am by nature a forgiving and compassionate person. I am also a male with a female slave, and that causes some additional issues. I was raised in the United States where, in the 1970s and 80s, "good men" were trained to believe:

- All women are my equals and should never be treated as submissive.

- Never raise a hand to a female.

- Always say: "I don't know dear; what do you want to do?" and "Oh, no dear, that dress doesn't make you look fat at all."

I was raised that the way to interact in a relationship was to capitulate and to lie. This is still reflected in our society and in the media.

I expect certain things from someone who calls himself a Master; one of the most important is how he responds to his slave's actions. As a Master, I am responsible for my slave's behavior. Her actions reflect on me. If she insults you, it is the same as if I insulted you. I own that action, and I need to address it by dealing with my slave who insulted you.

Recently, a Master/slave contest was held; Lady X and her boy y won the title. A few days later, boy y posted on a public mailing list that money from the travel basket was unfairly handled, that the owner of the contest was pocketing money, and "it just isn't fair." My first thought about that post was:

"How embarrassing for Lady X." After a few days went by without Lady X offering an apology for her boy's behavior, I thought: "How embarrassing for us all that Lady X and boy y won a Master/slave contest." (On a side note, the accusations were manipulative and unfounded; it's regrettable that such accusations were made public.)

We should address when it is time to assist in finding out what an issue is; how to make your commands clearer; and when you need to step up and address a potential problem. There will be times you should shrug and just say 'No biggie' if that's the truth of things.

But we must also develop our own set of boundaries, our own set of limits. What are your limits? What are you willing to tolerate from your submissive or slave?

There are times when we should be gentle and understanding—when illness, emotional distress, or life circumstances prevent our subs and slaves from serving us the way we know they are capable of serving—and other times when we must be responsible disciplinarians. This, too, is a duty— some would say a sacred duty—equal to leading our slaves toward positive growth, training them in serving techniques or other pleasing skills, or ensuring that they reflect whatever it is you want your slave to reflect.

Strength

Dan says...

As a Master, you must have a sense of strength. You will be looked upon as a leader and a source of strength. Operate from that place—"Sit in your seat of power." This does not mean you need to be arrogant, be a jerk, or lie rather than look bad; it does mean that you will have to work on your personal confidence. Confidence is the key to building your power, and a modest, humble sense of self-confidence is the most unshakable.

Any confidence that comes from your ego or from comparing yourself to others is doomed because you will find someone who is more skilled, handsome, etc., than you. The result will be that you will either falter in your self-image or lie to yourself to protect your ego. Circumvent those possible results by building your humble ego from within.

I can't tell you exactly how to build your self-confidence, nor will I try to be "Dr. Self-help" by chanting slogans ("You can do it! Dom that boy! Spank that ass!"). But know you'll have to address this issue because, when things become rocky due to internal or external forces, those you call slaves will be watching.

Demanding Performance

Dan says...

So far, we've painted a picture of a loving M/s household, where our slaves fearlessly and respectfully serve us. They do not have bad days, don't get sick, and never a discouraging word is heard...

Of course, this is not the way it always will be; we are all just human. Sometimes our subs and slaves are not on their best behavior, let alone simple good behavior. They act out, cuss us, and tell us to get our own damn shoes. A normally attentive slave forgets to do three clearly explained chores. A slave who is normally emotionally balanced and quiet responds with an out-of-the-blue, screaming "F* you!" A submissive who is well known for being cheery and happy moves slowly and without direction.

These things happen for a number of reasons, and a Master needs to make a proper response. It is our responsibility to do so, to keep balance. The quicker we respond, the sooner concerns are addressed directly, allowing us all to move forward. We need to develop the skills necessary to determine underlying reasons and to respond properly.

Physical bodies can, obviously, cause issues. It doesn't matter how long we've been in the lifestyle and how many people view us as Masters or slaves; we are all biological constructs. As such, there can be biological reasons why we are not at our best. Simple illnesses happen. We catch colds, have a bad reaction to food, have allergies, or have any of the hundreds of common ills we humans face. If we admit that we're dealing with physical issues, they are the easiest to deal with. If a slave is able to communicate "Ma'am, I hope you'll excuse my lack of attention because I have a head cold," we as owners can respond appropriately. I certainly can't fault my slave for moving slowly when she has a twisted ankle! The key to this issue is communication. If my slave is stubbornly trying to just "suck it up" and not bother me with the fact that she has a migraine that impacts her service to me, it's worse if I am unaware of the migraine and waste my time wondering about her lack of attention.

An entirely different example would be slave James forgetting to pick me up on time at the airport. After I take a taxi home, I would discipline him for the inconvenience and lack of attention to a known duty. Had slave James advised me prior to my arrival that he was suffering from severe insomnia due to a physical illness, my reaction (tone and discipline) would have been quite different. Hell, I would probably have changed the command from "pick me up at the airport" to "have me picked up," so as to not endanger either of us.

When my normally fit slaves are ill, I am pretty forgiving when their service to me is lacking—as long as it isn't a pattern or an excuse. If it does become a pattern, though, then it warrants my attention. Do I need to address my slave's physical care, nutrition, etc.?

As a Master, the key to dealing with a slave's physical ills is to ensure our property communicates details of their physical well-being. No matter what the ill, the slave must tell the Master.

There can be a problem here because some slaves may think that having a physical issue is a fault or a failure on their part. When a slave has serious physical problems, this can definitely be a challenge.

Emotional issues can also affect service. Whether it is our live-in, loving slave of many years or a service slave who simply cleans and cooks, emotions are part of being human. A Master cannot command emotions to be or not be; we can only command the slave NOT to hide their emotions from us, because that will cause the issue to fester.

A word of caution here: know your limits. If you are not a psychoanalyst or mental health professional, then don't take on that role. If my slave had a broken bone, I certainly wouldn't try to set it; I don't have that skill set. I would not try to counsel a slave regarding their depression or other serious emotional issues; I would instead require them to consult a professional.

There are also the day-to-day emotional challenges that impact performance. Annoyances at work, fear of rejection in a new situation, anger over the actions of other drivers, sorrow about the state of our environment, and no reason at all for general grumpiness.

As a Master, you need to develop an awareness of your slave; that will enable you to see when their behavior is "off." When you see that, respond. If it is an issue unrelated to your House or your M/s relationship, try this: have your slave stop whatever they are doing, ask them to kneel before you, and tell them to breathe. Their position can, of course, be modified, if required by their physical condition. Don't tell them to just "calm down." That counter-intuitive command might cause the slave to panic and wonder either if they don't appear to be calm or become defensive ("Can't you tell how damn calm I am??!!). Just instruct them to breathe and stay quietly with you. Then instruct them to be mindful of the current moment, stay within that moment, and realize that nothing else is happening right now. After a bit, tell them to return to service.

Depending on the relationship, you may ask them later about their day, giving them the time and space to share their emotional turmoil. Simply listening without judgment, without trying to fix anything, is a great gift. If the slave is simply a service or sexual slave, you might advise them to vent to one of their friends.

Discipline

Dan says...

Recently, my slave of 11+ years did something; I disagreed with her actions and responded. The following day, she politely requested clarification about what had been so displeasing to me. This is how the discipline and communication must work.

When I discipline my slave, the issue is resolved. If the slave has questions, let them come at a later point, when the focus of the discussion will be a desire to learn, not to simply engage in recriminations or self-blame. A Master must be able to act; in order to act, the Master must be confident. Acting in confidence leads to acting immediately and decisively. As you'll learn, a slave craves a confident, decisive Master.

In the example I gave, I analyzed the situation, disciplined my slave, resolved the issue, and moved on. When we later discussed the issue, I learned my slave's view of the situation, and it was different than mine. No Master, including me, is perfect or right all the time.

Correction, Discipline, and Punishment

Correction is simple: "You were instructed to do this, and you did not"; or "You did this, next time do that." Your slave did nothing wrong; you simply want to make a change. That's not a big deal and shouldn't be treated as such. Example: I am accustomed to my slave making coffee for me every morning and putting a cup of coffee on my desk. If she were to forget one day, having done it correctly 100 times before, I would simply point out that she forgot my coffee. It's a simple correction. Her action is to get my coffee now and remember to do so tomorrow. Issue closed. No big deal.

Perhaps I want my cup placed on a coaster, something I've never wanted before. The change of instruction is simple: "Continue to do what you've always done, and add one step." If she forgets the new step tomorrow, a reminder is in order. From a navigational perspective, you are just making a slight course correction.

In my House, we make corrections when necessary. After 11+ years with my primary slave, she knows me and my expectations pretty well.

In the beginning of a relationship, course corrections are more frequent, which is natural and expected. It's important both of you understand that correction is part of growth, not a sign of failure or a bad thing at all.

Discipline is different in that your clear expectations are not met by your slave, your commands are not followed, or your slave has made of habit of "forgetting" a command. Your reaction should not be a gentle reminder but rather a crystal clear message that your slave is failing to serve you. Yes, failure is a harsh word...but don't be afraid of it. This is an alternative relationship and, as a Master, our (reasonable) expectations are to be met. We put our effort into the M/s relationship, and we take on responsibilities; in return, we receive agreed-upon service.

The key aspect is to address a behavioral failure (to obey or to serve) while stressing that the PERSON is NOT a failure. That a specific desire, expectation, or command was not fulfilled is the failure to be addressed; address that specific failure, NOT the slave or the slave's overall existence.

My slave's behavioral failure may be ignoring the way I want my lunch packed, forgetting to address someone as I've instructed, or acting "catty" in public. For me, one such occurrence is addressed by correction; two are the start of an unacceptable pattern that requires discipline. These are failures to carry out my instructions. I address each one as an individual incident, not implying in any way that "you are a failure as a slave."

Discipline may be verbal, physical, or both; it might be humiliating or might be painful.

The first step is to bring the slave to a kneeling position and clearly express the nature of the failure. I don't want to hear any excuse—if my slave had a reason for the failure it should have been brought to my attention immediately before I do ("Master, your lunch won't have your favorite drink today because..."). My slave knows better than to offer lame excuses; if there is a legitimate reason, my slave presents it with respect in response to my question: "Do you have anything to say for yourself?" What I expect to hear is "No, Sir," or "I'll do better, Sir." The only other acceptable answer would be one I've heard before: "Sir, I believe you told me to stop packing apple juice because it gives you gas; did I misunderstand?" If that is indeed what you said, then admit it. Own your mistakes. Be confident you are doing the right thing—and own your wrongs.

After verbally confirming the issue with your slave, the discipline depends on the infraction. Here are some of my examples:

- If my lunch was not packed as I instructed, I might have my slave write 100 times: "One sandwich, one fruit, 10 pretzel rods, and a piece of candy."

- If my slave failed to address Bob as Master Robert, in accordance with my instructions, I would have her kneel in front of him while I apologized for my slave's lack of respect; then she would apologize. Believe me, this is VERY powerful.

- If my slave was being catty in public, she would be sent to the car to wait for me. When we got home, she would receive three quick strikes with a cane. A slave can enjoy/like/appreciate a caning for play; a discipline caning should NOT be pleasant.

Punishment should rarely be necessary. If you are frequently punishing your slave, there is a fundamental issue that needs to be addressed. It could be your ability to communicate with your slave, your slave's ability to understand your communication, you're slave's inability or lack of desire to serve, or your slave may be manipulating you to get your attention.

Punishment is required when my slave:

- develops an unacceptable pattern (regularly forgetting the same task, etc.);

- causes me or my House public embarrassment; or

- puts me, the slave, or others in danger.

For example, I would punish my slave for:

- posting derogatory or insulting things on a public message board;

- talking badly about anyone behind their back;

- engaging in unsafe play; or

- being inebriated to the point they lose awareness of their environment.

As with discipline, punishment begins by verbally addressing the situation, but in this case I am directly addressing the slave's failure. I often discuss the time I put into training, the actual or potential impact of their action(s), and why their behavior was not acceptable. After the discussion,

I will choose an appropriate punishment. My slave is much more impacted by having disappointed me than by any physical punishment I could choose.

Punishment should suck. It should address what the slave did and ensure the offending behavior will not be repeated. Privileges may be revoked, but the slave should know exactly what to do to earn the reinstatement of the privileges.

After Correction, Discipline or Punishment

Dan says...

Deal with infractions as they happen, then consider the issues closed and move on. If two days after the incident and my response, the slave offers another apology, I simply remind her we have dealt with and closed the issue; the best way to apologize is to ensure the issue never comes up again.

No matter what the incident is, address it and move on. Teach your slave that once you have addressed the issue, they also need to move on. Address it, and let it go.

dawn says...

I have heard many times over the years that if a slave likes caning or spanking, then caning or spanking can't be used as a form of punishment. I beg to differ. I have been caned for pleasure, and I have been caned for punishment. There is a difference. Caning for pleasure has a specific energy, an intent behind it—pleasure—that can be felt. Caning for punishment is the same in that it has an energy and an intent, but the intent is punishment. Caning for pleasure may or may not have a warm-up; caning for punishment definitely has no warm-up, and disappointment and displeasure are the emotions behind it.

For me, as well as most slaves I know, disappointing my Master hurts more than any physical punishment that could be given.

All Dan has to do is give me that sigh or that look, and I fold. The cane is almost welcome at that point because it helps me deal with my feelings and knowledge that I have disappointed him.

Like most slaves, I am a perfectionist, a people pleaser. One of the goals in my relationship is to please my Master. Failing to accomplish that goal tears me up inside. One of the first lessons Dan had to teach me was how to let go. I'm my own worst punisher, and I can make the punishment last for days, days, and more days. Dan taught me how to look at the wrong action, see that it was the wrong action, accept punishment for the wrong action, and then let it go. It was very hard, but that is a very valuable lesson, one I use in my entire life, not just within our relationship.

Transparency

Dan says...

It shouldn't be a surprise that I have access to my slave dawn's e-mail, instant messages (IMs), web profiles, and any other account or information I want. There is no reason for my slave to prohibit me from knowing anything in her life (with the exception of the occasional surprise birthday party). This doesn't mean I actually check her e-mail. It's been years since I've done so, and I don't really have a desire to poke around in her e-mail. I expect her to communicate to me everything I need to know, and I know that she will seek my permission prior to "hooking up" or playing with someone. My trust in her is so complete that I simply have no need to review her IM conversations or web accounts.

In our relationship, however, the reverse is true as well: she has a list of all my passwords, my bank accounts, my personal e-mail, my IM logs, and my laptop master lock password.

Our relationship goes far beyond passwords; I am transparent to her as a human. She knows who I am, what I have done in the past, the people I have screwed over, and those I have hurt; she knows my every fear, every button, and every regret. As a Master, it serves me to lay myself open and bare before my slave...and still be her Master. Despite everything I have told her, every button I've shown her, and every way she could get around my personal walls and defenses, she is still my slave. I am still the powerful force in our relationship. Being fearless of who I am allows me to wield authority. I am willing to hand the emotional equivalent of a loaded gun to someone with whom I will have power conflicts. I say: "Here is the gun and the ammunition; never use it"; I know she never will. Living in a glass house allows me to own my vulnerabilities. Was I to hide those weaknesses, keep them in the shadow, avoid exposing them to light, then they would wield power over me? Once a secret has been revealed, it can no longer be a totem of power against you.

Being transparent in totality to my slave has given me greater power over my slave...and even more power over myself.

Slave Training

Dan says...

One of the differences between a Master/ slave relationship and other types of relationships is the importance of and focus on change and growth. A Master's primary task is to bring his slave's behavior into line with his view of M/s and, depending on the extent of the relationship, to reshape their general worldview. This is commonly referred to as slave training.

This training could result in your slave asking the question: "What is wrong with me that you have to change me?" That's a flawed question, based on non-M/s relationship models. We draw a clear line between our power exchange relationships and other relationship models. Since I clearly take responsibility for my slaves' actions, then I am going to dictate the behaviors that drive those actions.

For example, I train all my slaves to behave in a certain way in lifestyle-friendly situations. I train them in proper protocols, attentiveness, and serving skills. Beyond that, I have spent time training slave jem to be more self-accepting and to understand the power of asking others for help. I've trained my slave dawn to be more compassionate and more confident. These lessons that serve me as a Master in lifestyle situations also serve me in general because I have stronger individuals surrounding me.

I have also trained dawn to become wet when she gives me head and not to have an orgasm without my consent. We wanted dawn to claim her sluthood, and these are valid training modalities helping us accomplish that goal.

Perhaps the first thing you'll want to identify is the purpose of your training. If you want a service slave, then you would teach (or require the slave to learn) Victorian service or the way to gracefully serve tea. If you're training a sexual slave, then orgasm control/forced orgasm/orgasm denial, and sexual health may be part of the teaching program. If you want a formal Leather protocol slave, then attend some Leather clubs or events, noting how slaves interact with Masters and with other slaves, where/how slaves stand, how they hold their hands, and when they refrain from eye contact.

While much slave training is individual and based on specific situations and results, there are some general aspects that define whether or not a slave has been trained. In my opinion, these are the minimums.

- Train your slave about appropriate displays of anger. Slaves are humans, and there will be times when they are angry: angry at you, angry at traffic, angry at the weather, or angry their sports team lost a game. A well-trained slave will never immediately display anger in public, especially not toward a respected member of the community. This does not prohibit righteous rage that is appropriate to a situation, such as abuse by one member of the community toward another. A trained slave will take a breath, keep their mouth closed, be with what they're feeling, and make a considered calm, directed response. A loud, angry slave is an out-of-control slave.

• Train your slave to listen. A well-trained slave will listen to you and to others, hearing the words that are spoken, and waiting to respond to a question until the speaker has finished (not even formulating the answer mentally until the speaker is silent).

• Train your slave to be mindful. dawn covers this is depth in her section about *Being a slave*.

• Train your slave to be respectful. A trained slave should approach everyone (Master, slave, or someone in the vanilla world) with an open mind and a respectful tone.

As with anything you yourself might be teaching, make sure you have the appropriate knowledge and that you walk your talk. If you go off in a foul-mouthed rage at the slow event check-in line, you're not the person to train your slave how to deal with anger. On the other hand, some things you can tell the slave to do the research, to find the appropriate class or teacher ("Slave, learn the Japanese Tea Ceremony."). You can then train them in other skills, such as giving them the penis they are being trained to suck.

There are many books and websites focused on training, and everyone has an opinion on the best methods, which may include ideas from motivational speakers or self-help gurus.

As a side note and a teaser: our next book will include specific training strategies for protocols, long-term relationships, slut training, and service slave training, to name a few!

(Editor note: That next book, Hearts & Collars, did indeed include all of this in-depth!)

Being a slave

Pride in Submission

dawn says...

Over the years when I'm kneeling before Master, taking his orders, or serving him, I've heard: "I don't know how she can do that," from those who don't understand M/s. For me, I can't imagine being happy living any other way. Yes, I submit. It doesn't mean I'm a doormat like some imagine. It means that I've looked deep within and decided that I want a relationship that is about growth— for both of us, by accepting our true natures. It is about embracing our desires and holding nothing back from each other. I want to be with someone I trust so deeply that I want to serve him. I want to be able to admit to and own my fantasies, having them considered and brought to life—if he so deems.

I don't want to be in a relationship where he asks for a cup of coffee and I tell him to get it his own damn self just because I want to be seen as a feminist or a strong person. I am a strong person because I've looked at who I truly am. I don't want to be in a relationship where he does the dishes by my side just because it's expected of him, just because that's the "official" standard to which he should adhere. I'd rather do the dishes myself, with pride in my heart because I know I'm serving him; if he's by my side, I know it's because he wants to be there.

Despite that, there's a part of me that's still afraid of what people will think when they find out that I'm a slave in my relationship. Some think that I'm powerless or broken. Some, even in the kink community, don't understand our relationship; I've sat down with a few of them over coffee to explain that in this relationship I am empowered, and the relationship is healthier than any prior relationship. "You have power?" they ask. Yes, I have power. Because of my Master's support and his belief in me, I'm able to do almost anything to which I set my mind. I have power; he has power—and he has control. So, although I have power, it is through his control that I experience that power, under his protection and guidance.

(Authors note: I use the term "doormat" a lot in this book, but doormat is not a bad word. Please see Erotic Awakening podcast episode 646 for a great conversation about this topic)

Slave as Property

dawn says...

When we first got together, we looked at the terms "Master" and "slave." At the time, those words didn't speak to us, so we didn't embrace them. We also knew that some were offended by those terms, so we set them aside and chose instead to use "Dominant" and "submissive." If you looked at how we lived, though, we were definitely on the Master/slave side of the coin.

Why do I say this? Because from the beginning, I was his property to do with as he pleased. I was completely subject to his desires. He owned me from day one. I found no greater pleasure than doing his bidding. Of course, there were times of struggle early on. Some days, I'd fall back on old logic, and up would pop thoughts like "Good girls don't do—or even want—this; what's wrong with me?" Dan would let me voice these fears, we'd talk through them, and then he'd make me do his bidding. Time and time again we would go through this process. I would walk into a wall of fear, he'd rip the wall down, and he'd make me walk through the opening. He would prove there was nothing to fear. And with each step, with each wall, he took down and made me walk past, I sank deeper and deeper into his possession.

I came to a place where I no longer feared being owned and used for someone else's pleasure. Instead, I craved it even more than I had when it was just a fantasy. The longer I lived as Dan's slave, the more I needed that life. I needed the knowledge that someone trusted me and wanted me enough to own me. Dan did not see me as a doormat. He knew that I was a strong person with a willingness to struggle through my fears, and he still wanted to own me.

Being "property" isn't like what I expected, based on fantasies. It's not all about being used sexually, though we still like to explore that piece sometimes. It's not about being ordered to do what Dan knows I want to do. I've had to do many things that I didn't want to do; things that were uncomfortable, things the purpose of which I didn't understand. My need to please Dan was so strong that I felt proud of myself for accomplishing a task he assigned me, whether or not I understood why he wanted me to do that task.

There are many examples I could share; I'll use one from the beginning of our relationship. Like most slaves I've encountered, at that time I only wanted to serve MY Master (remember that New Relationship Energy?); I didn't want to serve anyone else. They weren't MY Master, I didn't belong to them, I didn't know them, and I didn't know if I could trust them. I wanted to focus on my own Master's needs. The first time he asked me to serve someone else, I felt like he was rejecting me because I had somehow displeased him. He knew how I felt about serving others, and he started out in our relationship by being very possessive of me, and by protecting me. And here he was sending me to serve someone else. It felt like a punishment. The fear and trepidation in my belly took hold; I did not want to do it—yet, I would. Dan had his reasons, ones I knew he might or might not explain later. I had to learn how to breathe, how to stop considering "why," and how to move forward, completing the task with grace because what I do reflects on my Master. When I returned to him after serving the other Master, there was pride in my Master's eyes. I had walked through a fear; in truth, through a soft limit. If I remained in a place where I could serve only MY Master, that would limit how he could use me, and I'd no longer be property with total trust in my owner. Step by step, Dan pushed his property through the fears that can arise when you've handed yourself over to someone else's control and whims.

Seeing the pride in his eyes as I grew made me want to do more and more for him. What else could he make his property do? What other fears could we walk through together? Over the years, we have found many opportunities to show each other that we are owner/property, and we continue to do so.

My enslavement to him is complete. By working through these layers of fear and growth, I know that I would do anything that he asked of me. My questions of trust and faith have been answered time and time again. I am here to be used as he sees fit, and I crave the opportunity to do so.

The Collaring—Can I Do This?

dawn says…

It was not an easy decision to give someone that much control over me; I was terrified. I'm not a doormat, and in many areas of my life, I am a leader, someone who makes things happen. Yet, I craved the idea of totally submitting to someone else. While I didn't want to give up the idea of making things happen, I wanted my focus to be on making things happen for someone; creating something together; having him be proud of my successes; and helping me be proud of myself. If allowed the space to be who they are, Dominants can do this. When Dan and I tried little weekends of power exchange, I felt happy and carefree. I'm the type of person who is happiest when I know what the rules are because they've been told to me, and then I can follow them. When I'm disciplined for my slip-ups, I'm happy, knowing he isn't bottling anything inside. I do something wrong, discipline (as agreed upon in our contract) is dished out, and then we're done because the issue is closed. While not forgetting what I did, but not beating myself up over it, I can move on with my day.

I had a thrill inside at the thought of a relationship with this sort of intentional design. I must admit that I was also attracted to the naughty side of things. The main attraction to me, though, was that this relationship style seemed healthy because it is consensual, done with eyes wide open. Growth seemed possible in a relationship like this. I liked the idea of surrendering myself to someone who had earned my trust. I wanted to be allowed to be completely open and vulnerable to someone. I wanted him to be so trustworthy that I would follow him anywhere. I needed someone who:

- would not take advantage of me;

- seeing my potential, was strong enough to push me to be a better me;

- wanted to explore life with me in this manner, within a power exchange structure;

- was as naughty as I am;

- was willing to help me with my fantasies no matter how naughty they are;

- was willing to call me on my shit;

- was willing to tell me yes or no, based on what they wanted or knew was right or wrong; and

- made my heart and soul want to be about pleasing him instead of myself.

I wanted something I had never seen before, in life or even on TV. I wanted a man who was strong enough to take care of his woman while not suppressing her emotionally, physically, sexually, or intellectually; and who inspired my total support for his ideas, his goals, his sexuality, and everything about him.

This is what attracted me to the M/s lifestyle. This is what attracted me to Dan.

I also must admit to something I touched on above: the sexual side of this had me drooling. Although some M/s couples don't do kinky play, the kinky/BDSM side of M/s totally rocked my world. Being tied up, flogged, or spanked by someone in whom I had complete trust, and who found it hot that I'd surrender to him, was exactly what I wanted. The receiving of pain, the sensuality: it all spoke to me in ways I'd never before felt.

I wanted (and found!) a lifestyle and a man who can speak his desires to me; whose desires match or complement mine; to whom I can speak my desires and hear his growl in return; I know will take care of me, and care for me, during this process; who knows I have complete trust in him; and who knows I will follow his directions to the best of my ability.

It's hard to describe this experience to someone who doesn't crave a power exchange lifestyle. If you are nodding your head at this point, understanding what I'm getting at, imagining someone controlling you...perhaps you may be a submissive. If you like the idea of totally controlling someone, caring for them, and taking care of them...perhaps you're a Dominant.

I wanted us to build a structure in which emotional blackmail did not, could not, exist. The contract would be designed around the structure both Dan and I wanted, and we would follow it.

I wanted all of this, and the opportunity presented itself. Dan and I had been living what we called "D/s lite." This meant, that when we moved in together with the idea of trying a power exchange relationship, we did it in layers. We tried a little bit of this and a little bit of that, adding things as we went to see if the reality sufficiently matched the fantasy to be what we wanted. When the kids went to visit their dad for a weekend, we would become 24/7 for that period of time. We found that our craving for those weekends just kept increasing. Power exchange spoke to our inner cores. Right after moving in together, we became part of the local kink/BDSM community.

More and more, we became our authentic selves. In vanilla settings, I wanted to serve him, and he wanted to be served by me. When the kids were around, we were able to behave this way and all they saw was a loving relationship. We lived this way for over a year, Dan sliding a piece of leather around my neck when the kids were gone, going to munches and being around others, and creating/facilitating M/s support groups. One day, almost a year and a half after we began this journey of power exchange, Dan told me he wanted me to wear his formal collar; we were going to have a collaring ceremony.

We had never seen one before, so Dan had me do some research on ceremonies and contracts. He had me buy an "everyday" collar that would be engraved with the ceremony date; we chose March 3, 2001.

As we previously discussed, we created our contract. Then we had the collaring ceremony (which was a process in and of itself!), inviting some friends to witness the ceremony and celebrate with us. Dan and I were both nervous about taking this step, making this commitment—a commitment like neither of us had ever made.

The evening began, with me not knowing what my Master had planned. Once we arrived, he told me to strip down to almost nothing and serve our guests refreshments. Simple, right? Wrong. Up to this point, I had not served anyone else, nor had I been taught how to serve in that way; I had to guess at the process. Be unobtrusive; don't stand between the people who are talking; kneel when appropriate; don't interrupt; offer refreshments courteously when there is a conversational break. I was pretty much able to figure it out on my own (it's like being a gracious hostess, just to a VERY high degree!), but I was terrified that I'd make a mistake in front of Master's friends. I was on display, and everyone was watching me.

Well, despite my concentration, I made a mistake. Under "ordinary" circumstances, that mistake would have resulted in Dan correcting me and instructing me to redo the task. This though was a special evening, so when one of the Dominants pointed out my mistake, Dan acted as if my offense was a personal embarrassment to him (he later explained that he was testing me). Dan rose, grabbed me by the hair, walked me over to the offended Dominant, had me apologize to the Dominant, and then he apologized for my lack of manners and respect and then put me face down on the floor off to the side. Dan told me that I wasn't worthy to wear his collar; I was to remain on the floor until I had made a decision that I really, really wanted to wear his collar. The idea that I had messed up when I was trying so hard to do my best, that I'd embarrassed him in front of his peer Dominants, tore at my heart.

My position on the floor was out of the rest of the guests' sight. He left me there, alone, fighting my tears. A Master/slave relationship is not all fun and games. I knew this, but what if I couldn't do it? What if I couldn't handle letting him down? What if I wasn't strong enough to take my punishment when that happened? What if I wasn't worthy of wearing his collar? Feeling that I couldn't even get through the pre-collaring without embarrassing him, made my head reel with thoughts like "I can't do this."

Then, something shifted within me. If Dan didn't believe in me, he wouldn't have brought me this far, to this point. If he didn't believe in me, he wouldn't have me down on this carpet looking deep within myself. He would have canceled the party, thanked his guests, and taken me home. Instead, he chose to give me the chance to look deep into my heart and work things out in both my heart and my head before the actual ceremony.

I took a deep breath. This is what I wanted more than anything in the world. I could and would step through this fear, offering myself to him completely and without reservation. I stood up. I walked to the edge of the couch where only he could see me so that I didn't impact the energy of the room and the conversations. I held my hands behind my back and bowed my head, waiting to be acknowledged—if he desired to acknowledge me.

The conversation stopped; he softly told me to look up. I did so, gazing at him without fear. He nodded his head. He allowed me to approach the Dominant whom I had offended and offer a sincere apology. Then, Dan took off my leather thong from around my neck that I had worn for the last year and a half, tossed it across the room, and told me that if I still wanted to do this meet him downstairs in the basement dungeon. I had passed his test. At that point, I was very confident that I wanted to embrace this M/s relationship on a deeper level and I wanted it with Him. After a beautiful ceremony in front of our closest friends, Dan placed my permanent collar around my neck. To this day, I wear the collar that he gave to me that evening, engraved with: "Dan claims dawn, 3-3-01."

(Authors note: I still proudly wear that same collar)

Slave Qualities

dawn says...

We've previously covered many qualities that we believe a slave should possess or seek to possess. I'd like to emphasize the following qualities:

Obedience: I believe one important difference between a submissive and a slave is that a slave should reach the point of obeying her Master without question. The slave may want more information, but her first reaction should be to follow orders. Dan requires me to obey first and ask questions later. I know that he is looking out for my best interest. Of course, the exception to this would occur when you truly don't understand and you need further explanation. The question in your mind should not be whether you will follow the order but rather how you will accomplish the task.

Reliability: A slave must be reliable. A Master needs to know he can depend on his slave to do what needs to be done and to follow his orders. This knowledge creates trust in the relationship; trust that the slave places the relationship first yet, if anything happens to her Master, she can take care of herself.

Honesty: The power dynamic in an ownership relationship eliminates the need to play "games." In a vanilla context, we are discouraged from asking for what we want (it's seen as pushy and impolite); at the same time, we are equally pressured not to refuse someone else's desires (even if we believe doing so would be against that person's best interest or that of the relationship). Self-sacrifice is promoted as honorable.

In our relationship, my Master wants to know what I think and what I want. How can he make an informed decision if I'm not giving him the truth and the information he needs?

For me, this is very important in my M/s relationship. I NEED to be honest and to be held accountable. I don't lie, I don't fib, and I don't lie by omission. Because of this, He trusts me. Being trusted is a core need of mine.

Loyalty/Dedication/Devotion: My loyalty, dedication, and devotion to Dan were the result of the trust we had built between us. While trust is building, the slave should consciously choose to exhibit these qualities

Trustworthiness: A slave must be trustworthy. If the slave cannot be trusted, the relationship will never reach its potential depth.

Self-discipline: In my experience, most Masters want a strong slave, one who has self-discipline. If the Master gives the slave a chore, reminders should not be necessary. If she is learning something new, she should be able to focus on the task itself, without having her hand held.

Respect: Once trust has been established, respect should follow automatically. Without respect, it will not be possible to serve completely, to be vulnerable, and to be dedicated to the relationship. In the absence of respect, resentment will appear, and the slow decay of the relationship will begin.

Communicative: A slave must be willing to communicate her needs, wants, and desires. Again, how can a Master make an informed decision relating to the slave if he's not working with complete, correct, and honest information? A slave must also be willing to learn various communication styles as the relationship grows and changes.

Bravery: A willingness to face fears. Slaves will be commanded to do things that are outside of their comfort zone. Because of this, a slave must not only trust in her Master; she must be brave. She must be able to step forward, through her fears, knowing her Master has her best interest at heart. When it comes to sharing everything about herself, a slave must be willing to face her fears and walk through them. As I shared everything with my Master, I had to share all my memories as an abuse survivor. This can be very hard for anyone who has any kind of "secrets" in her past. I cannot stress enough how important it is to share everything. In order to make appropriate and effective decisions relating to his slave, a Master needs valid, honest, and complete information from his slave.

Graciousness: Throughout everything a slave will face, she must be gracious. A kind, charming, and compassionate slave will be one in whom a Master can be proud.

Slave Responsibilities

dawn says...

The responsibilities of a slave. Does anyone ever see or hear the word "slave" and wonder exactly what that means? Is she a doormat? Passive? Lazy? A people pleaser? Too weak to take care of herself?

Have you met me in person and wondered how I can call myself a slave? Don't worry; you won't be the first!

My role as a slave is the very basic foundation of my life and my M/s lifestyle. I am a slave and a wife; my Master is also my loving husband. This is my preferred lifestyle, the relationship style I choose. I've Topped on rare occasions, resulting in observers asking me how I can be a slave and be a Top. My answer: I am a slave in my core, topping doesn't change that. My core doesn't change when I'm organizing, leading, or running a group (or whatever); those actions I take have no impact on my core as a slave. No matter what, in my heart, I am still slave to my Master and everything I do is a reflection of him.

In my view of M/s relationships, a lifestyle slave needs to follow a strong Master, one who is himself a leader. Master Dan is such: a strong leader who has earned my respect. He and I live in a power exchange relationship. He leads; I follow. We have agreed upon those roles. We worked for a long time to figure out who we were and what would make us happy, then define it in a written contract. I would never have gone into this relationship lightly. I was giving up control, and he was accepting a higher level of responsibility than that to which he was accustomed. In return, I do my best to take care of him, and he does his best to take care of me—although, of course, we are each strong enough to take care of ourselves. It takes a strong individual to be a healthy, non-co-dependent slave. And what we wanted, and have achieved, is a relationship that is healthy, for us as individuals and as a couple.

As a slave, I have no interest in being a doormat or being in a place where I am unable to take care of myself. I like being a strong, empowered slave. We have heard a story told by a Master about his slave: if he left on a business trip, she wouldn't feed herself; he would have to ask other Masters to check on her and ensure she ate. To me, that is not a slave. A slave is able to take care of herself; she is the property of her Master and should be responsible for caring for their Master's property. That means taking the responsibility to keep themselves in a healthy condition. How can you serve if you are sick? If you purposefully refuse to take care of yourself, getting sick as a result, aren't you disrespecting your Master (and his property)? Others may feel differently; I know, however, that my Master expects me to be a strong woman. What's the point of dominating slaves who can't take care of themselves? Is that really dominating—or just enabling?

Whether I am a lifestyle slave, a submissive, or someone who only plays that role in a scene, I have responsibilities. This struck home in light of the following stories:

Take Judy, for example. She told me she played with Ann, someone new. Before their scene, Judy told Ann about safewords and how important they are. Afterward, Judy thought the scene went great...until later when Ann said that Judy's play was too hard for her. Ann never spoke up during the scene, even though Judy stopped several times to ask Ann if she was OK. [HINT: a safeword is a simple form of communication, given for a reason. USE IT WHEN NECESSARY! A new play partner has no idea what your limits are unless you speak up!] Judy told Ann that she had broken Judy's trust by not speaking up and, as a result, Judy would not play with her again.

John, a submissive/slave, told me he would never negotiate a scene or use a safeword. His decision. But then he whines that he didn't get what he wanted and that he didn't like what was done to him. He believes not negotiating or using safewords makes him a better submissive/slave. In reality, that just makes him someone who doesn't communicate and who will usually wind up unhappy...and so will the Top!

I was once involved in a scene with a new Dominant, so we first talked about what I did and didn't like. He said it was his first time Topping, and he needed to know my limits. I explained the way I use safewords and said he could use them to guide him as he explored my body and my reactions. The concept intrigued him, and he put it to good use. This new Dominant was able to stretch his wings because we used such a simple communication method.

One night at a Dom/sub charity auction I was "bought" by someone with whom I'd never played. After the auction, we negotiated a scene. I used the words "pain slut," and she asked what I meant. I said that I love where pain sends me, and I used to be able to take a lot of pain. She indicates that she likes bondage and asks if she can use bondage in the scene. I respond that I love the idea—as long as we stay in the public dungeon space. She understands that I'm Dan's slave and must work around his schedule, so we all talk about our schedules and set a time for our play. Immediately prior to the scene, she asks about my physical issues: I explain my tendonitis; she asks about my mobility, and I respond that, if I was sitting down, as she said she planned, I couldn't think of any issues. The scene begins. She binds me in rope, and I close my eyes, just feeling what was happening. She puts rope over my nipples; the rope hurts my left nipple too much to be enjoyable so, respectfully and softly, I let her know. She smiled and moved the rope a bit; I was able to close my eyes again. Then she sat me down, lacing me on the chair. Again, my eyes close as I lose myself in the sensations. She showed me the toys she planned to use, and I started to get excited. She inquired if I had a problem with any of them. The toys range from evil to sadistically evil; I'm OK with trying them all, knowing I can safeword if it gets too intense. I lost myself in the sensations, flying and soaring until— EEK! Whatever toy she used next was too intense, shaking me out of "my space." I didn't "yellow" (the "tread carefully" safeword) right away, hoping it might not feel so bad the second time. OUCH! It does. I like pain, but there's pain and there's PAIN. One more time. Nope. That was definitely a yellow. I called out "yellow," and she grinned...and switched toys. I believe she was testing me, and I passed the test, showing her I'd "yellow" if something was too much for me. That communication gave her the freedom to try more and more toys, pushing my limits. Which she did, over and over again. Very, very intense. And very rewarding. Communication is powerful, and it requires strength.

Please note that I've not been writing about play or safewords, per se. I simply used play situations to demonstrate good and bad communication. It is my job to: communicate what I need, express what I want, negotiate, and speak up! I am an empowered slave. I speak up, but I do so with respect. Dan and I have agreed as to how I'll speak up, and what style of communication I'll use. Communication: it's one of Dan's and my best qualities; it's probably one of the secrets to our longevity as a M/s couple!

Let's see...responsibilities include communication and strength. Can you take care of yourself? Does your Master have to hold your hand through everything you do? Can you survive on your own? In my case, I am a slave, and I choose and prefer to live in this lifestyle. It is not something that I MUST do in order to be functional.

If you are in a lifestyle relationship, do you have the strength to leave, if conditions so warrant? If something became very wrong, or if your Master began taking advantage of your gift of submission in an abusive way, could you walk away?

Do you have the strength to keep working on yourself, even though you are in a power exchange relationship? Your life is now about serving your Master, but do you also do things to grow as an individual? What happens if you, as a person, become stagnant? What do you bring to the table of your relationship?

Does your Dom/Master keep his side of the bargain? Unlike what some believe, a D/s or M/s relationship isn't just about the slave serving the Master. This is a power exchange, which means that BOTH parties must bring power to the table; BOTH parties have responsibilities.

Slaves have chosen to live in a power dynamic that most people wouldn't even consider. As a slave, are you living up to your responsibilities?

Doing Chores

Going as far back as I can remember, I never liked doing chores. Chores were an evil necessity, a form of punishment. Bad grades in school? Chores. Talk back? More chores.

Chores aren't fun, and who cares whether or not the house is clean? It will just get messy again the next day, especially when children are around. That was my general feeling, pre-Dan. My house was clean but very much on the unkempt side. No one helped me keep it clean, and it certainly wasn't appreciated when I made an effort.

When Master and I met and moved in together, my perspective changed. Neither of us liked chores, but we liked a clean house. We both worked full time and, now that they were getting older, the kids were expected to help around the house. It became very important to me to keep a presentable house for Master. He never had to tell me that he didn't want dishes in the sink in case he brought someone home. I knew that I would be expected to take steps to keep the house presentable… And it would actually be appreciated. Over time, I found that I started enjoying such chores. I can remember totally confusing Dan by putting something in our first contract under my "needs" section: I said that I needed to take care of his/our home; because I worked, though, I wanted his

help. I had figured out that I had a strong desire, a need, to keep his house in order. Because of my work hours, however, it wasn't possible for me to keep the house in order on my own, so I was asking for his help. Once I explained that, he did his best to understand the importance of my request. It finally sank in for him when he saw my daily frustration at not having the time necessary on an ongoing basis to organize, clean, and scrub everything that was needed. Ah, the joys of home ownership!

Over the years, we fell into a pattern. Luckily for me, Sir liked doing some of the household chores. He found cutting the grass to be very meditative for him. He loved to make dinner on the grill; that was a skill he'd not previously learned. Even though our division of chores developed into a routine, we both felt the importance of our needs and how we chose to meet those needs.

Then, I was laid off from my corporate job. We lost the house, the kids moved out, and we downsized to a small two-bedroom apartment. Being unable to find another job, I went back to school. Slowly, I began to take on more and more of the chores that Master had been doing over the years. Having the time to do these chores for him was a source of joy to me. One of his chores over the years was cleaning the cats' litter box; he never let me do it, and I was perfectly OK with that. He had a perfectionist way of cleaning the litter box, and it had been his responsibility for years. One day he told me I would be taking over that chore. This is going to sound odd to some: I felt honored that he'd trust me to do something in his perfectionist manner, even if it was such a minor thing. As a slave, I craved that kind of responsibility.

We present on many topics at kinky events, and Master began to turn over to me more of the admin tasks related to our presentations, including travel arrangements. Editing our websites and arranging interviews for our podcast, *Erotic Awakening*, were among many additions to my chores. Taking over some of the duties that had filled his time again made me feel honored.

Being a 24/7 lifestyle slave, doing chores and other tasks is amazingly fulfilling to me. I have purpose, I have goals, I fulfill my Master's desires—and in turn, this fulfills me.

The Joy in Giving

dawn says...

As a slave, I take great joy in giving my submission to my Master. I enjoy serving him and ensuring his comfort. My focus is on him and his needs, which allows me to let go of my ego. I know some women who are offended when their husband asks them to do something he could easily do for himself; they seem to believe he's just lazy (which may, of course, be the case). For me, however, I'm honored when Dan asks me to do something for him, especially if it's something he can do for himself. He knows that I crave serving him; by assigning tasks to me, he recognizes my need to serve and fulfills my desires. My Master is s strong man who can easily take care of himself. Therefore, my serving him is an honor.

There are many things that I do for Dan during the day. I wake up when he does, but since I know he needs a few minutes of private time, I remain in bed for about 15 minutes or so. Sir prefers room-temperature coffee, so I make a pot of coffee before we go to bed every night. When I get up, I get his vitamins and a glass of water for him. While he reviews his e-mail, I pack his lunch and prepare his clothes for the day, along with packing his gym bag. I love starting my day focusing on him and his needs. I concentrate on each chore, doing them with mindfulness. When I take him his vitamins, it's because I want him to remain healthy, not because it's an assigned chore. When

I lay out his clothes, it's because I want him to look his best. When I pack his lunch, it's because I want him to enjoy a tasty meal. I think about each of these chores, these rituals, with mindfulness. My focus is on Dan, and on the service itself.

This has a way of setting aside my personal ego. It's not about me or what I'm getting from performing service. It's more a form of selfless service; there's no promise of reward. Dan is aware of my actions, and my service, and he regularly says "thank you." But his thanks are not the reason I provide service. My goal as Dan's slave is to please him by my service and my actions; and these actions please him.

As part of the background, allowing a slave to be of service to her Master helps build the foundation of trust. Dan trusts me to perform to his required high standards all the duties he's assigned. In return, my trust in him is greater because he trusts me.

Mindfulness

When asked what the most important skill is that I've learned as a submissive/slave, I'd have to answer that it's mindfulness; being in the present moment with my focus on what is at hand.

Once I learned about, embraced, and began to serve with mindfulness, I became aware of how much of my life had been spent mindlessly, without awareness. With each effort I put into our relationship and my service to Dan, I am mindful of what I'm doing and why I'm doing it. Although the "why" isn't always at the forefront of my actions or thoughts, the "what" is definitely primary.

When I make our bed every morning, I don't just straighten the covers. Instead, I think about my Master and how this pleases him. I remember his command that I make the bed in the morning, and I pay attention to the details of what I'm doing. As I serve his coffee, I'm not a wife pouring her husband's coffee; I'm a slave who has the honor of serving her Master. I make his coffee as he likes it; then, with intention, I serve his coffee, mindful of my demeanor and tone. Do I just hand him his coffee as I pass by on the way to my computer? No. I stop, wait for him to acknowledge me, look him in the eye, and bow my head to him as I place the cup on his desk. When I take off his socks at night or put on/take off his boots, I stop talking, take a breath, calm the chatter in my head, and concentrate on the experience of what I am doing. I feel the texture of the socks or boots, the energy of our connection, the heat of his skin, and the sound of our breathing; everything else stops and that moment becomes primary. This is an example of mindfulness as opposed to mindlessness. Were I to perform these rituals in a mindless fashion, of what use would they be? What purpose would they serve? In my mind, the actions would be useless and mindless. There is power in mindfulness; there is a connection in mindfulness. When I am serving my Master, I want nothing in my head other than the service I am providing him.

Something that has been a major help in this endeavor is my experience with meditation. When participating in any kind of meditation, and especially mindful meditation, we learn how to slow the mind down. When we slow the mind down, we are able to focus on the 'now.' It's in the 'now' that we are able to experience the moment we are experiencing. In the 'now' we are able to be mindful of what we are doing. In the 'now' we can be present to the service we are providing, whatever that may be.

The idea of mindfulness and increased awareness has been critical to my growth as a person and as a slave. At first, it was quite a challenge because we were so accustomed to multi-tasking. If I failed to be focused, Dan would remind me. Now, it is part of what I do when I'm serving him and for the rest of my life. Mindfulness has led to a personal transformation in my life not only as a slave but in my life in general. I am grateful that, so many years ago, mindfulness is one of the first skills Dan taught me.

Honor as a Slave

dawn says...

What is honor to me?

Honor is about right actions and right speech. When acting with honor, we feel a sense of rightness and peace within ourselves.

When we act with honor, we treat others with respect. We do not gossip about them; we don't lie about them. We do not allow the politics of any group to sway us in our honorable treatment of others. Honor is about being helpful to others as we strive to be the best person we can be. When we are our best selves, we are honorable. Honor is not just a concept; it's how we interact with others.

As a slave, my actions reflect the honor of my Master. If I act wrongly in the "vanilla" world, in the

lifestyle community, or toward another individual, I dishonor myself, my Master, and my House.

Transparency

dawn says...

Recently, the importance of transparency came to the forefront of my attention. We've discussed this concept over the years with others beginning their M/s journey, and I can clearly explain the importance of transparency in our lives. Sometimes, though, it's easy to forget just how important something is until you're put on the spot by being asked a direct question.

When we ran for (and won) the title Great Lakes Master/slave, a question from the audience was put to me: "Do you require transparency in your relationship?"

I thought for a quick moment, and I'm not sure the following answer made sense to the questioner: "No, I don't require transparency as a slave, but he is my Master because he is transparent in all that he does." Several judges nodded their heads as they made notes, so I think they understood what I meant.

I was trying to convey that I had never formally put in our contract the need or requirement for transparency. But when Dan and I talked about our backgrounds prior to moving forward with a M/s dynamic, we had both been betrayed by others' lies.

Because of our past, and our knowledge that we had each been harmed by those lies, we wanted a completely transparent relationship. It's not an easy route to take, nor is it a M/s requirement. Transparency reflects how Dan and I choose to live.

Deciding to be transparent can make you very vulnerable to judgment. Transparency means not hiding anything. There have been times I've done something for which I knew I could be punished, something Dan might never know about. I couldn't keep it secret, though, because it would not only eat away at me but at our very foundation that we had worked so hard to build. So I'd share it with him, ready to live with the consequences. Sometimes he would punish me; sometimes he wouldn't see it as important. But, either way, I knew he would treat me fairly, understanding how difficult it sometimes was to share, especially if I'd already judged myself.

Dan is transparent as well. As a Master, how transparent should you be? Dan may not explain to me why he does what he does, but neither does he hide anything from me. There have been times when he's sat me down to tell me something that otherwise could have impacted my trust in him. Instead, his transparency increased my trust in him. He took the risk of telling me, of not keeping it a secret. That clearly demonstrates how important our relationship is to him.

Transparency is one of those concepts that are difficult to explain to those who don't understand a loving M/s relationship; it may be the loving part or the power exchange part they can't understand. Some believe the slave should share everything. For me as a slave, though, I need my Master to be willing to share everything with me as well. Mutual transparency goes a long way toward strengthening that foundation of trust.

For me as a slave, I NEED to be transparent and I NEED my Master to totally believe that I am sharing everything, telling him everything about myself. I don't ever want him to think that I'm keeping secrets. The idea of holding back, of hiding something potentially disrespectful or hurtful, makes me die inside a little bit. I NEVER again want to live my life within walls, terrified my secrets will come to light. I much prefer shining that light myself, by my choice.

Alpha Slave

dawn says...

Although Dan has from time to time said that I'm his Alpha slave, lately the term has taken on a new focus for me. Formerly, it just meant that I was his permanent, primary slave of long-standing. When he brought other slaves in, they understood that not only was I his slave, I was his wife and they were to respect me as such. Still, he treated me as his slave.

A while ago, Dan decided to take a different path with me as his Alpha slave. He was bringing in a new slave for training, and he required that I help with her education by teaching her how to serve Dan. In the past, he hadn't required service from others; they were more like submissive girlfriends. He trained them, but not in any specific, organized way. The new slave, however, was going to be a House slave; I would need to guide and teach her. Mentoring a slave of Dan's was a new role for me, requiring that I draw on my personal experience in mentoring others in the community, being a slave, and, particularly, being Dan's slave.

I wasn't certain I could do this; I would be expected to take the lead in some aspects of her training, giving her directions and commands. I had to learn and become comfortable with little things, like sitting beside him instead of on the floor, with the new slave sitting at "our" feet. That was a challenge because I love sitting at Master's feet; it felt very odd to have someone sitting at MY feet. This, however, was the way Dan wanted it, and he supported me as I worked through my emotions.

In addition, I understood what he was doing: he was pushing me, and helping me grow. After ten years of being his, he was creating another scenario, one that required my growth. That was not the main reason he wanted her in a relationship with both of us, but it was why he wanted me to learn these new skills. He had faith in me, faith I could master (so to speak!) these skills, even though this role was not my preference. I was somewhat frightened by the whole idea; Dan, however, takes his role as MY teacher and guide seriously. He helped push me through my fears, knowing I'd be OK in the long run.

Over the past year, I've had to learn new behaviors, including how to sit next to Dan instead of at his feet and to release my hold on some services I consider "mine," like serving his coffee. His decision to change my role a bit was the right decision because I had inadvertently begun to cling to that service. Clinging to something, then having that something changed, causes pain. I suffered when those services were taken away from me. I knew in my head that I hadn't done anything wrong and that I was not being punished. Master was simply showing me I did not have possession of my service to him. Despite my knowledge, it felt like punishment or rejection, and I had to look within myself, trying to determine why I was being punished. Utilizing self-talk, I worked through my feelings and figured out why he was making these changes. In case you haven't yet figured this out about me, I'm a "why" person: I NEED to know why things happen.

I figured out the why of my being trained NOT to "sit at his feet" and NOT to "serve his coffee." I realized doing those things doesn't make me a slave. They don't make me HIS slave. Once I fully understood, both knowing and feeling that understanding, my strength again welled up, and it was easier to be his Alpha slave. I was able to:

- sit next to him and point at the floor, reminding her to sit at his feet

- show her how he likes his coffee

- how to serve tea

- answer her questions when she was confused

- and teach her to obey without asking "why."

That last one, not questioning, is always a difficult lesson, but I could at least share my experiences.

Although I resisted taking on the active role of an Alpha slave, Dan's requirement that I do so absolutely made me grow both as a person and as a slave. Once again, my Master proved that he knew what he was doing, and that what he did was truly in my best interest. Even though the road during this period was tough, I've definitely come out the other side seeing how I've changed and grown. I see the power of our relationship. I see how the actions, and the service, don't make me a slave; they are ways of displaying who I am. Instead, my slavery is what's in my heart; that is where my true self resides.

I've also come to understand all the work Dan puts into our relationship. I've understood it before, but not on this level. Since he has me direct the new slave on occasion, I've come to understand the work involved with being a 'capital letter type'. Maybe, since he IS a Master in his heart, Dan doesn't see this as work, but it definitely takes thought and energy. Despite my gaining skill in this, it still doesn't draw me. I can command and lead, but there are many more skills needed to be a great Master. I am still a slave; now I'm a slave who has a greater understanding of both sides.

Slave vs. Priestess

dawn says...

I've surprised people on both sides of the fence, referring to the spiritual and the M/s sides. Come to find out, though, there really doesn't have to be a fence. Some who meet me in my role as a Priestess are surprised to learn I'm a slave; those who know me in the M/s world are sometimes taken aback to discover I'm a Priestess. I can certainly understand the confusion; hell, it confused me for a while, too! Obviously, though, it's possible...because I'm doing it!

Many years ago, I was asked by the President of the National Leather Association-International, Rafe, to officiate his leather wedding and collaring of his slave, Dee Dee. He wanted the ceremony performed by someone within the Leather community who was legally able to perform a wedding. He was a bit concerned about my ability to handle such a wedding because I was a submissive/slave. But I fit the qualifications since at that time I had been officiating weddings for over two years, I am very skilled at it, and I thoroughly enjoy performing weddings and commitment ceremonies. To help calm their fears about having a submissive perform the wedding, they wanted to meet with both me and my Master. When we met, Rafe (as was appropriate) addressed Dan, who stated I would be speaking on my own behalf.

Both Rafe and Dee Dee were visibly relieved to hear I had a voice. Their confusion had been understandable because Dan and I had been living "high protocol" for the previous year, so that's how most people were used to seeing me. When it came to weddings, though, that was my skill set, and Dan didn't involve himself unless necessary. By the time the dinner meeting ended, they were confident I could do the job to their satisfaction.

When others in the community learned I'd be doing Rafe and Dee Dee's wedding, Dan was continually asked if he thought I could do it and those in our M/s support group kind of giggled. Although that surprised me, I was OK with it. I guess they didn't know as much about me as I thought they did! Before becoming Dan's slave, I was in charge of many things: I ran the PTA chapter at my son's school, creating and leading projects; I started the school's Cub Scout troop and led all four grades until the following year when I had trained other parents; I ran fundraisers for various organizations. Why would that change? After becoming Dan's slave, there was still a core piece of me that needed to be created and led. I created a spiritual group that I ran for over six years, and I helped Dan run several D/s support groups. Early in our relationship, I found my spiritual path and became clergy in that path. I specifically wanted to be available to those in the alternative lifestyle communities. Following my training and ordination by my tradition, I was licensed by the state of Ohio.

Through all this, I had the support of my Master. He believed that I could lead, run groups, create things, and be a Priestess, all while being his slave. With his belief, I believed, too.

Back to my story!

I performed Rafe and Dee Dee's collaring and Leather wedding, receiving many compliments (and some tearful ones!) from the guests. I had put to rest the fears and questions about my ability to perform ceremonies. After the wedding, wearing my Priestess robes, Dan put my leather collar around my neck, fastened my leash, and had me kneel at his feet. There was no doubt that I performed that ceremony as his slave, as a reflection of him.

Many people assume a slave is merely a "follower," and I think that's one of the reasons some have difficulty understanding my ability to be both a slave and a Priestess. I'm familiar with a number of slaves, slaves who prove that assumption is far from the truth. Slaves are strong; slaves are organized; slaves are leaders. It's just that we slaves find our power by surrendering it to a Master. We find our strength by giving ourselves to a strong Master, someone we admire, who can

guide us and give us the structure we need. Because of the structure of our M/s relationship and the guidance I receive from my Master, I am able to be my authentic self. My authentic self is both a slave and a Priestess.

Today, I officiate at weddings and funerals; I create and lead rituals for my spiritual group; I run workshops on sacred sexuality and energy work. I've led the energy group for SMART, a BDSM group in Cleveland, Ohio. I also kneel at my Master's feet, knowing he is proud of what I'm doing for the community as a slave and as a Priestess.

Our Community

Your Neighborhood Community (M/s, BDSM and More)

Dan says...

No matter where you live, there's probably a local kinky community. The number and variety of groups may, of course, depend on the size of your city. When we first became active, there were two groups in town—a generic BDSM group, and a chapter of the National Leather Association (dawn just mentioned the NLA in connection with her first Leather wedding; their website is www. nla-i.org). There wasn't a local group specifically for D/s, M/s, or power exchange relationships— or any other "alt" for that matter (just to clarify, there were gay Leather groups, but we didn't know about them then).

Times change, and today in my hometown, you can't swing a flogger without hitting a local kinky group of some sort!

But why bother with groups at all?

Early in my power exchange relationships, it was very important that I surround myself with like-minded people. After all, we were entering into a lifestyle that most people rate mildly strange, at best, to truly sick. Being around others who had similar views on punishment, the need for consistency, or why Master needs a day off on occasion, I was able to open up and explore who I was, without fear of being judged. Yes, there is value in online interactions; however, nothing can replace seeing other people living the lifestyle. The example they set, as well as the explanation of their relationship—even just the verification that power exchange relationships can and do exist, is critically important.

I mentioned online interactions; there are sites like CollarMe.com that assist you in finding partners. FetLife.com introduces you to people and groups that let you argue about what to do once you've found those partners. I have found that both CollarMe and FetLife offer good forums, places with good people where you can bounce ideas and questions around or where you can find assistance and answers...if, of course, you are willing to wade through some not-so-valuable stuff (otherwise known as "crap"). How much of actual value will you find? Don't ask me; go look for yourself. Post an opinion or question on either side, and in return, you'll get opinions, different opinions, more opinions, arguments with those opinions, and possibly be slammed for posting the original opinion or question. Sometimes it's worth wading through some shit to get something of value. If you can do that and not come out smelling like shit, all the better!

For now, though, we'll keep our focus on the real-time community. I mentioned that our hometown of Columbus, Ohio, has seen an expansion from one or two kinky groups to more groups and more varied options. Columbus isn't a small city, but neither is it known as a Mecca of kink. Let me tell you about a few of the Columbus groups; this may give you an idea of what your community might have to offer.

- *Group One*—A BDSM-centric munch group that has been around for ten years. Munches are dinner-type social gatherings in public venues; they provide time for old friends to gather and newcomers to learn about the community. That's pretty much all Group One is about.

• *Group Two*—A D/s lifestyle support group that has also been around for about ten years. This group's focus is on people who are involved in power exchange relationships.

Pretty good, so far. Two groups whose different formats serve two different kink communities. As the commercial says "But wait, there's more!"

• *Group Three*—A generic fetish group. Mostly focused on BDSM but open to other elements. This is a really popular group because they throw play parties! Although not core to living M/s, play parties are important for many people for socializing, finding play partners, and playing (and they're fun, too!).

• *Group Four*—A TNG ("The Next Generation") group for younger folks (between 18 and 35) who are interested in Topping, bottoming, or both. I don't have much to say about this group because it's fairly new...and because I'm a day or two past the age 35 cutoff. I've been accused of being jealous. Am not!

• *Group Five*—A group dedicated solely to bondage, people being tied up with rope. Period. It is not unusual to have special interest groups dedicated to a single craft or kink. The first-ever play party we attended was held by a spanking group.

This list is certainly not complete! We run a group of people who chat about M/s. There's another group exclusive to cross-dressers. There are a number of gay Leather groups in town. Plus two new groups have been created since we started writing this book!

Whoever you are, wherever you are: you have LOTS of choices. Find a group that suits you, or create your own. On a side note, if you find a group that seems to be run poorly and you think you could do a better job...go do it! (Not the first time you attend, though!) Don't stand around and bitch, get involved and do something!

M/s in the Kink Community

Dan says...

Foremost, we are Master and slave in our personal relationship. M/s takes place in our home, and it is who we are. It not only reflects how we live physically; it shows in our hearts and our actions as well.

When we travel, when we are in public spaces, our power dynamic doesn't change. However, when we're around the "vanilla" public, most of us choose to express our power dynamic in a more subtle way so as not to draw attention to ourselves and our non-standard lifestyle. We don't want to frighten anyone or cause others to be uncomfortable. We want respect for our choices, so we must be respectful of the more standard world.

When we are at events or involved in groups that focus on kink/BDSM rather than the power exchange lifestyle, we still get to express our authentic Master and slave self. And there are a number of good reasons for TPE couples (or triads or Houses) to visit the land of kink. We might enjoy the BDSM activities available at events or local dungeon clubs. Or we travel to events to attend the classes, workshops, and discussions that frequently include not only BDSM skills but often involve relationships, spirituality, polyamory, etc. We attend local munches in order to socialize with friends and meet new people who are trying to find their place in our lifestyle.

While some events are solely for women, gay men, or a particular fetish, the majority of larger events across the country (make that "across the world"!) are considered "pansexual." That means EVERYONE is welcome, without regard to biological gender, chosen gender, sexual orientation, or kink. As you explore that general pansexual alternative lifestyle community, you'll notice that we who follow a path of a total power exchange are in the minority. Many who identify as Dom or sub are actually making reference to the role they fill when they play. This in itself is neither good nor bad; however, it can be overwhelming. The desire of a TPE M/s couple to fit in and be accepted within the kink community can sometimes be a challenge. I've heard it compared to being in a peer group of 30-plus-year-olds and you're the only one with children. Everyone else is focused on fun, deciding who'll make the next beer run; you're having fun...but you have one ear on the baby monitor. Sometimes we Master/slave couples are considered uptight. My slave can't just sit with "the girls" and rag about how stupid the Tops are; I can't just ignore my slave's behavior, shrugging and saying "Girls...what'cha gonna do?"

I'm not implying that TPE relationships aren't fun—they are; but it is also a lifestyle with responsibilities, just like any adult life. Don't be confused (or discouraged) by those responsibilities. Responsibility itself is not just about work, and it's not a bad thing; it is a balanced thing. When you live responsibly, accepting responsibility, it flows into who you are and how you act. As such, it is amazingly rewarding.

Because the kink community is so large and easy to find (compared to a strictly Master/slave group), I feel that Master/

slave couples have a responsibility to be who we are, open and visible, within the kink community. I'm not suggesting we be "in your face" in the kink community, nor do I think we are "better" than "regular kinksters" (we're not). We need to be visible to those who, after enjoying a nice flogging, think: "That was fun...is there anything more to this stuff?" Those folks need to see the alternative option of M/s as a lifestyle.

This is how dawn and I got started—a BDSM munch group gave us a chance to meet like-minded M/s people...and away we went!

Leather

Dan says...

I once attended a discussion group regarding Leather as a lifestyle (not "leather working," not "leather wear," and not "the material my flogger is made of"). The group leader asked the attendees whether or not we considered ourselves "Leather." When I responded that I didn't consider myself Leather, he seemed quite taken aback. But before we explore that—and how I would answer the same question today—let's back up a bit.

I'm not going to expound on Leather history; there are better books as well as more knowledgeable sources. What I've learned from others is that this lifestyle originated with male veterans returning to the United States after World War II. Men who appreciated the structure, the look, the camaraderie, and the "manly men" they had served with formed motorcycle clubs; they were very much gay male groups. The history of Leather as a lifestyle is interesting and worth some reading; I recommend a book by Steve Lenius: *Life, Leather, and the Pursuit of Happiness* and a visit to The Leather Archives & Museum located in Chicago, Illinois, or to their website, www. leatherarchives.org. Decades passed, and today those who identify as "Leather" include gay men, lesbians, heterosexuals, bisexuals, and transgendered—in other words, pansexual (all genders, all orientations). Of course, some groups still have a single gender/orientation requirement.

There are differences between modern-day Leather groups and kink groups. Although this difference is hard to describe, kink groups tend to focus on activities or fetishes. Leather groups are about Leather as a lifestyle, often focusing on history, ethics, responsibility, integrity, honor, and respect.

We'll talk more about these same ethics later in the chapter on M/s Ethics. Although the core ethics are similar, not all Leatherfolk are into M/s, and not all M/s couples/families/ Houses consider themselves "Leather."

As I began this section, my reason for saying that I was not "Leather," as well as the difference between my M/s House and a Leather House (or even a Leather M/s House), can be summed up in one word: tradition. I felt that we were not formally recognized by the Leather community as peers and, as a result, we didn't have the right to use the word "Leather."

The history of Leather is steeped in tradition. Entry into the community sometimes followed specific rules and structure, much like ranks in the military. However, in today's online world, one can choose one's own title by selecting a screen name ("Master_Awesomesauce," "slavetoall," etc.). While the ease of finding information online is good...perhaps the informality of choosing your title rather than having it bestowed upon you by your peers is not so good. Of course, many in the Leather, kink, and M/s community have indeed earned the titles they use...and many are self-determined, too. Who is real and who is an "Insta-Dom (just add computer)" isn't always readily apparent.

In Leather, you are granted your title, following the traditions. You "earn" your Leathers in various ways. You are given the title "Master" when your peers recognize you as such because of your beliefs and your actions. A Master's Cover (usually a black leather cap with a visor) is formally presented to a Master who has been recognized by his peers; being given your cover is a high honor.

As an aside, I was recognized as a Master by a member of our local National Leather Association many years ago. Later, dawn and I entered a contest and were awarded the title of Great Lakes Master and slave 2010, representing a 13-state area. More recently, I was honored by a Covering Ceremony, in which I was recognized as a Master by the community and received my Master's Cover from my slave dawn. Although this was a wonderful tribute, I had already self-determined my right to the title of Master. I know what I have done, what my training has entailed, what my ethics are, and where my heart lies. I know who I am: Master Dan.

After I told the group I didn't identify as "Leather," the others in the room—my Leather peers— talked with me about my answer. They reviewed with me who I am and what our House is about. They reminded me that my mentor had recommended I start a chapter of MAsT ("Masters And slaves Together"), which is a M/s discussion and support group. Basically, they told me I "damned well" was Leather and I should just "stop arguing." As I've said, I don't require their approval in order to validate me or our House...but it does, of course, feel good to be acknowledged by one's peers.

I spent many years in a very healthy M/s relationship that had no involvement with the Leather M/s folks; you may decide that's what works for you. I certainly don't suggest that getting involved in the Leather community is a good idea for everyone or that you need a Leather title as validation of any kind—I really do not believe either of those things is necessary. But I do feel strongly that it's always a positive thing to look at options, so see what the Leather community has to offer, find out why they make such a fuss about earning or gifting Leather, and why they honor traditions. Then decide if the Leather community will bring value to your life and/or your relationships.

Mentoring

Dan says...

If you join an online group and post that you are a submissive new to the lifestyle, plenty of "Doms" and "Masters" will offer to "mentor" you. That's not what we mean when we speak of mentoring; rather we mean peer mentoring, something in which we place great value. We believe that the best mentor is one who has had similar experiences, someone who has been in your shoes.

Reading some of the classic lifestyle books (those by Guy Baldwin, Dossie Easton, Molly Devin, and Jack Rinella come immediately to mind) is a great way to gain knowledge, online resources offer opinions...but you may find information that's conflicting or simply doesn't apply to your life. If at all possible, it's much more helpful to be able to go to an individual who can say: "Yes, I've been there; here's what I did and how it turned out."

Mentors don't tell you what to do; instead, they share their experiences and lead by example. In a D/s or M/s context, a mentor will assist you as you explore this lifestyle. They should be someone who has been around for a while and who has had some of the experiences you might encounter. A mentor must be someone you can trust. As you explore yourself and look into the mirror, you can go to your mentor and say: "Look what I've discovered; what do you think?"

In my opinion, mentors are most effective when they are your peers. I've heard of Masters who mentor slaves, but to me, the more accurate description would be to say they are training a slave or acting as an advisor to the slave.

Masters, Mistresses, and Dominants are best at mentoring other Masters, Mistresses, and Dominants; submissives and slaves are best at mentoring other submissives and slaves. To us, the logic of that seems straightforward; if a slave is uncertain about why a Master is doing something, talking to another slave can be a safe way to share concerns or doubts. When sharing an issue with your Master, as you should, they may help you with obeying and following through, but Only another slave can say: "When that happened to me, my experience was..."

And the opposite is true: there is no reason that Masters and Mistresses should not rely on each other for support. Too often we "capital letter types" may be more concerned about how others will perceive us instead of concentrating on the reality that being a Master or Mistress is a full-time, serious responsibility.

One example we've used to explain our view of peer mentorship is that of a pilot and a flight attendant. If you were new to either job, to whom would you go for advice? As a new flight attendant you could, of course, ask the pilot's opinion on how to do a task or why something is done a particular way...but, really, what good would that do? The pilot's experience is with his/ her own job, which is flying the plane. So, would you rather ask someone who might guess the answer

("Well, if it was me, I'd probably..."), or would you ask someone experienced in the task at hand, someone who can say: "When that happened to me, this is what I did..."?

To us, that's why we think peer mentoring in the Master/slave world is the way to go.

I Am a REAL Master, but YOU....

I tend to avoid most online M/s (or other lifestyle) chats or posts because they too often dissolve into rants, tirades, criticisms, and mockery. A simple question gets a simple response...followed by a request for clarification, a post about something read in a book, an example where the author of that book said he didn't like fish, a cheer of support for those who hate fish, a rebuke to those who post about fish, and finally someone who says plaintively, "Can't we all just get along??"

These posts, though, are at least honest bashing, which is much less annoying than bashing and gossiping about someone behind their back. That's the unfortunate aspect of being involved in any way with real-time communities.

I've been a bit taken aback, and I've laughed more than a bit, at some of the things I've seen and read. My favorite is someone who enters the scene and goes, in a week's time, from "So, this is a munch?" to calling himself "Master Painmeister" and representing himself as having "15 years in the lifestyle" (because he played "cowboys and Indians" at age 12 and once tied up another kid). It's a challenge not to poke fun at that person, not to be offended because you were a slave for a year, learning "from the bottom up" before you were allowed to call yourself a Master. This practice was far more common within "Old Guard" Leather M/s, but it's rarely seen in today's practice of M/s.

But…remember that you're also looking in a mirror; at least I was. Since I wanted to be accepted, I came up with a cool scene name (OK, I thought it was cool), played the "I knew I was kinky when I pulled Suzy's hair in pre-school" card, grabbed a BDSM toy and came out swinging. I didn't even really know what was meant when someone yelled "RED! RED!"

Fortunately for me (and the bottom involved), observers stifled their laughter, gently removed the crop from my hand, and offered to help me by mentoring me. They could have mocked me, reacted with sarcasm, or tried to score "cool points" by deriding my skill (or lack thereof). Instead, they understood they had an opportunity to lead and teach, and they acted responsibly to help bring out the best in someone new.

When you see someone screw up, make a mistake, or imply a level of expertise they don't possess, you'll have that same opportunity. Will you turn on them, slam the door, and practice your witticism by making sarcastic jokes about (or, worse, to) the "stupid newbie"? Or will you laugh with them and say: "I remember doing it that way, and it didn't work out very well. May I make a few suggestions?"

Most of us who have received helpful assistance when we stumbled our way into the lifestyle are more than happy to "pay it forward," making the choice to ease a new person's journey.

Be an active part of your community. Stand for what is best within it. You'll get good reactions because healthy people who want to grow and learn will be attracted to you.

Regarding group gossip, politics, and assholes...they'll always be with us. What you can do is NOT engage in such behavior. Ever. (If you do, it will come back to haunt you.) As the Master of a slave, not only lead by example but do not allow them to engage in that behavior, either.

Time in the Lifestyle

Dan says...

There is a comment I frequently hear that I find unnecessary and, to some extent, annoying. It begins with "I've been in the lifestyle for 30 years" and is usually followed by "I knew I was kinky when I tied up my (or "my sister's") Barbie doll."

It seems to me that tying up a Barbie doll is not an indicator of your future kinkiness; I'd be willing to bet that many a Barbie doll has been tied up by average, vanilla, heterosexual kids! I honestly think if you were raised in a normal, healthy household, anything you did pre-puberty would not be an indicator of your post-puberty sexuality. Many people disagree with me on this; they point out that they watched a movie at eight years of age that showed someone tied up, and they immediately knew they were destined for kinky life. So, since there are many conflicting opinions, perhaps I'm wrong. Just take this as my opinion.

That aside, most of us consider "time in the lifestyle" to be time spent actively engaged in living this as a lifestyle. The clock doesn't start running when you jerk off to Betty Page (or Betty Boop, or whatever); it starts when you actually engage with other individuals, exploring and exercising your kinky self. Of course, if you say that a solo research project made your heart race and got

your cock hard or your cunt wet, I'd be likely to cut you some slack. Think about someone telling you "I've been playing the violin for 20 years" and you discover their experience consisted of buying a violin 20 years ago, taking it out of the box 10 years ago to take two lessons, and then 10 years later showing up at the symphony hall...would you consider them to have been a violinist for 20 years? I sure wouldn't.

Personally, I used to pull the heads off my GI Joe action figures and throw them down the laundry chute. In the unlikely event I become famous for decapitating actual humans, I could just say: "I knew my destiny when I was 11 years old because..."!

dawn says...

What about time spent in an online "Master/slave" relationship? Should that be counted? Having spent a short bit of time doing online M/s, I must say they are two completely different experiences. They are so different that I, personally, don't count online time as "time in the M/s lifestyle."

There are many reasons I personally discount this time. To begin with, how can you be part of a M/s dynamic if you don't even know for certain to whom you are typing? Who is that person on the other keyboard? It could be anyone. How can you develop a relationship of trust if you don't know the person or look into their eyes?? They could really be who they say they are...but it could be a man pretending to be a woman, a woman pretending to be a man, a 50-year-old sitting in his mother's basement claiming to be a hot 25-year-old, or a married person acting without spousal consent.

When online, if a "Master" told me to do something for him and I didn't want to, I simply didn't do it; how would he know?

Even if he learned of my deception, what could he do about it? Of course, he could ignore me by not logging on. Then I'd just jump into another online chat room and find someone else's online collar to wear simply by putting a { } symbol after my screen name.

If I didn't want to participate on any given day, I just wouldn't log into that chat room. When in a real-time M/s relationship, that's not an option. You have to deal with life on a face-to-face basis, interacting with another human: a live, warm human being who has feelings and expectations.

Here's an example: your online Master tells you, as a sign of respect when you talk with him, to sit on the edge of your computer chair, not allowing your back to touch the back of the chair. You type, "Yes, Sir," as you slouch in the chair. What's going to happen to you for not following the command? Not a damn thing. Now picture your real-time Master telling you to sit upright on your chair, not resting your back against the chair. When he sees you slouching, do you think there will be real-time consequences? You bet! Master just might come up behind you, grab you by your hair, yank your head back, whisper into your ear, "Why are you disobeying my order?" Not waiting for your response, he pulls you out of the chair, by your hair, pushes you to your knees, and begins to chastise you.

Big difference, hmmm?

Online is a whole different world than real-time. Going from one to the other means you have to start at the beginning and learn a whole new skill set on how to work with a slave, gaining real-time experience.

Yes, I know there are those who disagree and that's OK. This has just been my experience.

Your M/s

What Does M/s Look Like in YOUR Home?

Dan says...

Both annoying and great is that there is no "one right and true way" to have a power exchange relationship. It's annoying because no book, including this one, will be able to provide you with step-by-step instructions for what to do in order to be successful in your M/s relationship. Your life, your experience, your needs, and your desires will direct you to doing what works for you and your relationship.

The great thing is you can modify what you learn into a form that best suits you. dawn and I decided early on (prior to signing our contract) that, outside of our relationship, we each wanted to explore love and our own sexuality. So we knew we were interested in both swinging (casual, intimate, sexual encounters) and polyamory (more of an ongoing relationship). We found we made rotten swingers and did better at polyamory—after some hit-and-miss experiences. But many M/s couples never take the path of sexual exploration, never add a third, and may never even play outside of their primary relationship. That can be the basis for a power exchange relationship that's just as valid and wonderful as any other.

The following sections will offer much information that you can sit back and reflect on as you picture what YOUR M/s relationship may look like. As they say, "Take what you need; leave the rest." But whatever options you choose, make sure you build a strong, healthy foundation. Once that's in place, you can pick and choose among the possibilities to create the décor that perfectly suits your relationship.

Rituals

Dan says...

Now I'm going to suggest you institute some rituals in your life and your M/s relationship. Rituals are habitual things we do, with intention, to ensure we remember what is important to us. You might think that rituals (such as in religious rites, workings, or something else) are, or must be, very complex. Really, though, simply kneeling before an altar, prostrating oneself before the Buddha, or calling the quarters are all we need to do to bring focus and mindfulness to what we are doing.

In your busy life, rituals will help keep you (and your submissive/slave) on track. When life is going well, they are like soft, comforting touches. When things are bad, though, rituals can remind each of you what your focus should be. Your rituals ought to be relatively uncomplicated, not take too much time, and have some level of interaction. Make sure your rituals have understandable meanings (i.e., know why you are doing a particular ritual) and add value to your life. Don't just do them by rote; do them with awareness and purpose.

The number and type of rituals you use on a daily basis is up to you. Don't make the rituals turn into work. A Master can assign tasks and work to the slave, and sometimes regular tasks or chores can become rituals. It's the intent behind the task that transforms a simple task into a beautiful meaningful ritual. They are relationship-empowering habits just waiting to be formed.

In the example below, it may appear the slave is the one doing everything. That's not the case; the Mistress must also play her part, bringing full focus to the ritual in order to acknowledge whether or not the ritual has been followed correctly. It is the connection between the slave and the Mistress which gives the ritual power.

This is an example of the daily rituals performed by a slave for his Mistress:

- Before his Mistress awakens, the slave arises and prepares the coffee. When she wakes, he brings her cup of coffee, prepared just the way she likes it. He kisses the cup and wordlessly hands it to her. Making eye contact with her slave, the Mistress nods and accepts the cup.

- Mistress leaves for the day, as usual, and the slave remains at home, also as usual. The slave writes an e-mail to his Mistress, specifying the items on his "to-do" list for the day. The slave begins each item with: "If it pleases you, your slave will..."

- Upon the Mistress' arrival at home, the slave kneels removes each shoe, and kisses each foot.

- As they prepare for bed that night, the slave first asks his Mistress for permission to sleep in the bed (even though that's where he always sleeps).

dawn says...

When creating rituals, make sure that they have meaning for both of you. One of our daily rituals is my serving Dan his coffee every morning; this is meaningful to both of us. In Dan's previous marriage, his wife refused to serve anyone coffee, feeling it was demeaning to her and stripped away her power; Dan remembers hearing me respond to that tale by telling him it would be an honor for me to serve him his coffee. So for us, it's a very poignant and beautiful ritual. Ensuring he has his coffee is my initial daily task. Therefore, my very first act each day is a ritual that reinforces my submission to him. After all these years I still hand him his morning coffee with reverence and mindfulness. I not only serve his coffee, but I serve it with graciousness.

There are a few rituals that I do during the day. Remember, these are just examples; you need to find what is right for you and your relationship. Since I'm now working from home, I love doing things that help my Master prepare for his day in Corporate America. I organize his gym bag, knowing I'm contributing to the maintenance of his health. I lay out his clothes, knowing what he's wearing will be a day-long reminder of my service. I pack his lunch, making something he'll enjoy and adding a surprise treat. Not only are these rituals done out of love and service, but they also allow him to have some time by himself in the morning before he leaves for work.

Although I have other rituals throughout the day, the ones I love the most are at night. When Dan comes home, he sits down and allows me to remove his shoes. I get to sit at his feet and slowly, mindfully, take off his shoes. I get to massage his feet. I get to connect with him. Then, I wash my hands and serve dinner. Later at night, I serve him ice cream, and then I undress him for bed.

These are our rituals. Just to keep things fresh, sometimes Dan may make minor additions or changes. For me, though, whatever he has me do is an honor. I not only love the rituals, but I love that our relationship is important enough to him that he incorporates rituals into our everyday life.

Farming Your Relationship

Dan says…

In talking with two friends just starting a M/s relationship with each other, I tried to share with them the need to balance the active process of building the relationship with the passive concept of simply letting the relationship take its course. Think of it as cultivating the relationship; when you think of cultivating, think of a farmer.

The farmer tills the soil, seeds it, waters it, and perhaps feeds the crop. Then he keeps an eye on things, making adjustments as needed. If the crop grows slowly or isn't coming up "just right," the farmer doesn't flash-burn his farm. He adjusts his thinking and keeps working while at the same time accepting that the crop won't always grow the way he'd prefer.

So, once you've done what you believe you need to do, step back and let your relationship grow at its own pace. Learn from your mistakes, and keep moving forward.

As you can probably tell so far, I take power exchange relationships seriously, and they do, indeed, take a lot of work. They need adjustments and maintenance; like the farmer, you must be willing to get in there and get your hands dirty. But remember: once you have made a correction, attended to an issue, or adjusted an aspect of the relationship, it's time to step back and let it grow.

Believe that you have created a strong foundation; let the clay dry, and the cement harden. Have faith that you have made the right start, a solid start. Stand back and become an observer.

There will be times when everything is fine, and times when life may not be great, but it's definitely not in chaos. Sometimes we forget that "if it ain't broke, don't fix it." We forget that sometimes all we need to do is stay out of the way.

I've found Masters and Doms sometimes have a tendency to jump in and "do something," when what needs to be done is...not a damn thing. We sometimes feel that, since we've put so much effort into the relationship, we can't let our attention stray from it for a single moment. As Masters, our sense of ownership and—let's face it—our need for control can sometimes result in our trying to fix that which is not broken. In fact, by trying to keep everything functioning at 110%, we can actually push things out of balance. Too much tinkering can cause the exact problems that you're trying to avoid.

Sow your seeds, then leave them in peace, allowing their growth to happen. Remember: a power exchange relationship requires a lot of work, so if it's moving along at its own pace, take a breath, and take a break!

dawn says...

Using Dan's analogy of a farmer sowing and watching over his crops, keep in mind that, even though you're watching the field and allowing nature to take its course you don't get to ignore the field. Even when everything is going according to plan, a secure environment is necessary to ensure continued growth.

Some maintenance may be necessary to keep the edges from eroding or to keep the weeds at bay. These maintenance needs should be noticeable; the more experience you get, the easier it will be to spot those pesky insects, weeds, and erosion.

Your Children and Your M/s

Dan says...

A wide range of philosophies exist around living in a full-time power exchange relationship when you have children living at home. One end of the spectrum is "We don't tell the kids anything, just like we don't tell them what we do in the bedroom; it's just not appropriate or necessary. On the other end of the spectrum, which we don't support, a woman posted on a kink forum mentioned she had been raised in an openly M/s friendly household; now that she was "of age," her stepfather wanted her to become his submissive. She posted that she felt a bit funny about this—as well she should.

Of course, deciding exactly what you want to share with your children, how much or how little you want them to know about your M/s relationship, is up to you—to some extent. I've met more than a few folks who said they had been raised in an openly M/s household; from what I've seen, I suspect this number is not going to decline. There's an important caveat to consider as you make the decision about what to share with your children: some parents chose to be age-appropriately open with their children, who told the stories to their friends, and those friends told their parents... and then the police arrived, and the M/s couple lost custody of their children. (Support the NCSF—The National Coalition for Sexual Freedom. They can help with child custody and other issues. Their website is www.ncsfreedom.org.)

I'm going to share with you my experience raising children in a power exchange household and offer some thoughts for your consideration as you make decisions for your home and family.

Regarding the previously mentioned girl and her stepfather, in my opinion the stepfather's behavior is, at the very least, completely inappropriate and, at worst, abusive. If the girl's mother, who is her husband's slave, hasn't yet thrown her collar at him as she threw him out, she needs to step back, ask herself what the fuck she's doing, and take action to protect her child.

In our case, my slave became my wife, bringing into our home her two sons (both of whom I'd known since their birth. We decided that the kids didn't need to know we were in a power exchange relationship, and they didn't need to know we attended BDSM parties. What they did need to know, what they saw and understood, was that their mother and I were in a loving relationship and that I was the ultimate authority. They learned we were open to people in non-standard relationships, and they knew our friends included gays, parents of gays, transsexuals, heterosexual couples, and other non-average folks. We made no obvious references to M/s, and the kids had a clear understanding that we didn't hide in the bedroom, fight and argue, or throw things.

What they saw was that we acted ethically, had certain expectations of each other, and smiled a lot. They knew we were an "open book," ready to answer any questions they might ask.

As the boys got older, they would occasionally come across things that gave them pause; sometimes they'd ask questions. One borrowed the car and found a cane in the back seat; another asked where we were going when we went to "events," and they wondered why the guy in the National Leather Association float at the gay pride parade flashed us and yelled "Hey, Dan and dawn!" Sometimes they'd ask, 'Uh, what?'. We always answered, though on occasion dawn was challenged to come up with an age-appropriate response!

You'll need to find that balance between protecting and not hiding who you are. Children, like adults, don't want to hear lies. However, sometimes you need to play the tried-and-true answer: "Because I'm the adult, and I said so!"

Parenting is a difficult task. Finding your way, finding the balance, and raising your children to be healthy adults can be the most challenging of tasks...and the most rewarding.

Build Your Own Community—YOUR M/s House

Dan says...

I live by a certain set of beliefs, ethics, and opinions about what healthy M/s looks like, and my slaves share this view. As I began to mentor peers, we discussed our views, saw they were similar, and thus was born House Metta. The dictionary definition of "metta" is: "lovingkindness, the Buddhist virtue of kindness," and we use that word as it refers to selfless service. Our goal is to allow one's nature, be it Dominant or submissive, to flourish in a protected environment as well as to live the three core principles of House Metta: Respect, Honor, and Growth.

We created our House as a place that allowed the safe, authentic, self-expression of Masters, slaves, Dominants, and submissives. It provides a space where we can gather in a M/s setting to share our ideas and experiences, as well as our questions. It's also a "Leather Family," a Tribe...like-minded people around whom you can be your authentic self and trust they will be there for you.

The creation of such a House, a Leather Family, and a Tribe, makes it possible for others of like mind to find you. It's of great value to you as well, being supported by people who believe in what you believe, and see what you see.

Below are some of the core concepts of House Metta. We did not recruit nor invite; like minds, attracted by our philosophy, just showed up, saying "Hey, this fits us, too!" Slowly, our House expanded.

Here are some of the ideas and values of House Metta:

- Skills and protocol can be taught, but they are merely tools that allow you the freedom to be a submissive, a slave, a Dominant, or a Master. You cannot simply step directly into these roles without preparation, just as you cannot attend college without having first attended kindergarten, grade school, and high school.

- Through mentoring and House association, we at House Metta provide a safe environment in which individuals can explore alternative sexualities. Our information is honest and up-front.

- Regarding training, I (Dan) take this seriously. I am not in it to get laid or to get play dates. I have no ego to stroke nor desire to have either a harem or to play. I am satisfied with the slaves I own. This allows me to train submissives without any expectation of ongoing service to me; I simply expect them to become their personal best as a slave or submissives who will be associated with our House for as long as we both feel a mutual fit.

- Responsibilities: We strive to make House Metta a valuable resource to its members and to the community in general. Being a member of our

House has privileges—as well as responsibilities. Those responsibilities have evolved and been outlined as a result of good ongoing internal communication among the members of our House.

• House Metta Values: In our daily lives, we are personally responsible for handling ourselves with dignity and integrity, because our actions reflect not only on ourselves but also on our House and its members. Be who and what the House stands for by being your authentic self, and act accordingly.

• Group Politics: It is important to not get involved in community/group politics unless you are actively responsible as one of the group's leaders. You are part of House Metta; what you do is a reflection on the House, its leader, and its members. If community/group politics interests you, be an active leader, not a spectator who tosses out opinions without offering to work on the necessary changes. Keep in mind that not all groups need to change—if you want to do something different, create and lead a new group.

• Drama: Avoid unnecessary drama. Use positive reinforcement. Never speak ill of others outside the House, unless relates to those who prey on our community. In that case, though, take care not to base your judgment on half-baked "facts." Balance your responsibilities to the community with the concept of "innocent until proven guilty," knowing that every story has at least two sides. Simply advise caution rather than making proclamations about someone.

• Community: Take an active part within the House. If you have knowledge or skills, share them. Educate others when appropriate, and be involved with our community. Be a visible presence, allowing seekers to see the many available options in our lifestyle.

Finally, I believe it's best to run a M/s House as a benevolent dictatorship. Since I am not the Master of all the members of our House (especially NOT of the other Masters!), it would not be appropriate for me to issue commands. However, I am responsible for running the House. I seek input, discuss issues, listen to questions and answers, consider different ideas—and then I make the decisions. As long as my decisions continue to serve those in House Metta, folks stick around. If/when my decisions cease to serve, members may decide to create their own House; that would be fine. House Metta moves in a clear direction, with "politics" kept to a minimum. Running a House is NOT the same as running a group, nor should it be.

Finding a Third

Dan says...

One of the more common posts you'll see on lifestyle-friendly online sites is: "Master and slave seek another to join our household." Now, from here it takes different tracts: "Slave should be female/male/gender unimportant, be willing to relocate/available on certain weekends, and be height weight proportional/looks unimportant", and so on.

For a variety of different reasons, power exchange couples who don't identify as monogamous may decide they want to add another person to their home. Some couples do identify as monogamous, but they may not see the addition of another slave in a House as a conflict. Some reasons for bringing others into your M/s relationship are probably better than others.

At times, it is simply a matter of logistics. The Master may be trying to reduce the workload of an existing slave or he may be changing the existing slave's focus, wanting someone to complement his slave and encourage her to grow. For example, bringing in a new slave to focus on the housework chores, could allow the other slave(s) to return to school or put their energy toward a career outside the home. Sometimes the Master needs to have additional "manpower." I know of one Master whose in-house Leather Family is large enough that he needs two slaves dedicated to housekeeping and another who focuses on administrative chores.

Of course, there's a different (potentially great) reason for adding a third: sex! Sex can be fun and exciting; there's nothing wrong with it being a part of your M/s household. Sex slaves (male, female, transgender, etc.) certainly exist; they not only fulfill your naughty, deviant desires but, in so doing, they fulfill their own. We don't need to outline all the obvious benefits...but, because it is sexy and naughty, let's do it anyway! I think of having a male slave I can command to mount my female slave while, at the same time, I'm caning his ass and commanding him to fuck faster/slower/ stop/go; watching two bisexual slaves playing for your pleasure; "forcing" a bi (or "bi-curious") slave to service someone of the same sex; having two slaves service you while commanding Slave One to remain silent while commanding Slave Two to make slave One moan. Oh, the ideas are endless!!

There are other, more practical, aspects of having sexual slaves in the House. If you have a gay male slave and a straight male Master, perhaps having live-in (or visiting) sex slaves for both of you can be interesting. Not to put a damper on sexual ideas, but sex drives change. My desire isn't quite what it was 20 years ago, but my primary slave is as horny as ever!

As I said, having an additional slave, sexual or otherwise, can be fun, exciting, and rewarding; there's nothing wrong with that scenario. HOWEVER, you MUST be ethical about it. Although we've dedicated a chapter to M/s ethics, it bears repeating here: if your offer to a slave is sex and nothing more, BE CLEAR that's all you're offering. It's not uncommon to find a slave who thinks that sex is a door into a broader relationship, so it behooves an ethical Master/Mistress to be completely transparent and extra-clear when you make an offer. Ethics are always important; as a Master seeking to add someone to your primary M/s relationship in any capacity, you have increased responsibility for all parties involved.

You may seek to bring in a third for the relationship aspect. Companionship, love, and a desire to incorporate others into a healthy relationship are all valid reasons for growing your House. The basis for this may be selfless or in your self-interest.

Some individuals call themselves Master or Mistress simply because they like to be surrounded by a herd or a harem. They think that collecting slaves reflects their greatness and desirability as Masters and Mistresses. They say: "Hey, look at ME: I have FOUR slaves wearing MY collars.

That means I'm pretty awesome!" Ugh. That's ego talking, not the words of an ethical Master. If you need to prove how great a Dom you are by pointing to your skill at collecting slaves, all you're really proving is that you can draw slaves to you (perhaps "suckering" them in with false promises?). The value of a Master/Mistress is not measured by the number of their slaves. Of course, not everyone who has more than one slave is simply a collector. But I know of very few Houses with one Master whose multiple slaves grow as people or stick around for more than a short time.

So whether you are a Master or a slave, I highly recommend you move with purpose—and caution—when seeking to be or to find an additional slave.

Oh, and by the way, while we're on the subject: if you're a slave who gets turned on by the smell of Lysol and sits around thinking: "If only I could find a Master who would let me clean all day and all night...," call me, OK?

M/s in a Vanilla World

dawn says...

Once we have embraced the M/s lifestyle, many of us find it difficult to live out in the vanilla world. In the beginning, we may be under the misunderstanding that our actions are what make us Master and slave.

We wonder how we can be ourselves in the vanilla world because: we can't be on our knees serving our Master at a restaurant; we can't wear a heavy leather collar to work; and our Master can't carry his flogger on his belt at all times. That behavior would create a "non-consensual scene" (it would involve vanilla observers). And what about around our families??

For me, my slavery is in my heart. My actions reflect on my Master, but that doesn't mean that I need to be overly dramatic or be the center of attention. Our lifestyle doesn't need to be put on display around those who don't understand. Of course, I'll keep an eye on his glass, ensuring he doesn't run out of his beverage. I may hand him his napkin or do something else to show him I'm aware, and taking care, of his needs. I don't need him to command me or have me kneel before him in a vanilla setting. Adapting our behavior to be appropriate to the setting doesn't hide who we are; it shows respect. Besides, we know that our Master/slave relationship lives in our hearts and souls.

One day someone asked what my kids thought about me being chained to a recliner all day. Huh? My brain froze; I had to think about that one. Someone who had known me for years actually believed I spent my days chained to my Master's chair?? In front of my kids?? In front of their friends?? Why on earth would someone think that? Oh, yes; that's right. That's what they've seen on television. No. That's not how it works in real life! At home I serve my "husband" with mindfulness, showing him kindness, graciousness, and respect. At night I sit at my husband's feet, and my kids think that's cute. What they see is a husband and wife in a respectful, loving relationship. There's no need for anything else.

Besides, it's the little things. I usually walk slightly behind Dan; sometimes it's because I walk slower, and sometimes it's because the M/s energy is flowing and making the right, respectful choice. There are a lot of little things like that, things that go unnoticed in the everyday world. In the end, though, it's not our actions that make us Master and slave. That dynamic lives in our core, and it expresses how we relate to each other.

Some Will Never Understand

dawn says...

Most people in the vanilla world—even some in the kink community—don't understand M/s relationships. They simply cannot fathom either how one person can surrender completely to another, or how one person can take responsibility for another. They can't comprehend the benefits of either of those roles. Naturally, in our sex-obsessed yet sex-negative world, some can well understand the erotic appeal of playing out these roles in the bedroom...but the whole lifestyle thing? Weird, man; just plain weird.

As I've knelt before my Master I've overheard: "I don't know how she can do that. I would never let a man have that much control over me." As I'm seen serving him I've heard whispers of "If he was MY partner, he'd be getting his own damned drink!"

They just don't, or can't, understand, because it's so far from their way of life. I feel cherished when I kneel at Dan's feet. I assume they think I'm being oppressed, which is most definitely NOT the case. He's not forcing me, not physically keeping me from leaving. I'm not brainwashed, and I'm not co-dependent. At his feet is where I prefer to sit. Dan does a lot of work and expends a great deal of energy being a Master; sitting at his feet is a sign of my respect, and respect for who he is and what he does, for me and for us.

Why does anyone, female or male, believe that getting a drink for your partner makes you weak? It saddens me to hear "You can get your own damn coffee," or something like that. If you're supposed to be in a loving relationship, why wouldn't you be willing to get your partner a drink, especially if they ask politely? In my case, I've chosen to be with a partner who not only appreciates my serving him but one I love to serve.

I can actually (and sadly) understand some of the reactions I've written about. I've been in relationships where I didn't want to get my partner a drink. But I hated feeling that way, feeling like I had to stick up for myself so my partner wouldn't take advantage of me (that chess game thing). But Dan, my Master, doesn't take advantage of the power I have given to him; instead, he uses it to help me reach my fullest potential, knowing that's my true desire.

I want to be in a relationship that has a M/s structure. As I've said, it's the most healing and empowering relationship I've ever experienced. For me to reach this level of surrender required that I have complete trust in my partner, that I show my true self, and I be completely vulnerable. I had to share all of my secrets, something I'd never done before because I never had the opportunity to trust the right person.

It was a major undertaking for Dan when he decided he wanted to be my Master. First, he had to teach me, to prove to me, that one person—Dan, himself—could be trusted. He accomplished that goal by being trustworthy, time and time and time again. We've been together for over a decade, and he has not broken that trust. (He's human, of course, so he's gotten a bit close once or twice!) However, I know that his code of honor is strong, and he would never, will never, do anything on purpose to break that trust. He knows what effect that would have on me, and our relationship means too much to both of us.

To learn that I could trust a man with my heart, my emotions, my dreams, and—literally—my life, was a huge turning point on my healing path. I've surrendered to him, and he's demanded things of me, things that might frighten me but that I chose to do for him despite my fear. Coming out on the other side of that fear without harm has shown me that life isn't such a scary place after all, because Dan has my back.

Those who say "I'd never allow that," don't know what they are missing! Or, maybe they do; maybe they think they have complete control over their own life, and, deep inside, they're terrified that control just might be an illusion.

I also believe that some people just aren't wired this way, making them truly unable to understand. In that case, I can write and talk, expounding on the benefits Dan and I gain from our power exchange relationship, but it won't matter; they just can't comprehend. That doesn't make them "bad" people; we simply don't have a common language. If I could, though, the one thing I'd want them to hear and believe is that I AM NOT A DOORMAT, and Dan is not an overpowering ogre. I am where I want to be, and so is he. We complement each other. He requires me to be a strong person and follow my dreams, while at the same time being vulnerable. I require him to be a strong person and follow his dreams, while also remaining vulnerable. We each have different roles in this relationship, roles we've chosen and designed with mindfulness, and we're both happy with the choices we've made.

In the end, though, either of us can choose to end the relationship. We can do it dishonorably by just walking away, or we can do it honorably by following the steps we've outlined in our contract. As we've said, we designed an exit clause going into the relationship. It wouldn't be an easy process to follow our plans and end our relationship with honor. But, then, should it really be easy to walk away from something so important and all-encompassing?

Friends have worried that, no matter what happened, I could not leave Dan. However, I know my own strength; I know I could leave, were the cause drastic, major, irreparable, and insurmountable. Our relationship is important to me, important enough to roll up my sleeves and work with Dan to get through whatever might happen.

Back when I was in my early 20s, a co-worker used to talk about how her husband would make her dress in a sexy manner and then take her out to the mall. I don't think she could have put a name to their relationship style or even really defined it. She did say how much she enjoyed it, though! I found it intriguing, but some of our female co-workers were appalled. They eventually talked her into leaving her husband, telling her he was treating her "wrong." They failed to hear her say how much she enjoyed what they did, and they were unable/unwilling to see the glow in her eyes when she talked about it. Just listening to her made me tingle at the thought of being in such a relationship. So those women who didn't understand, couldn't believe the relationship was consensual, pushed and pushed her, eventually destroying a relationship that was a positive thing for this woman. (Peer pressure is very hard to resist, especially when we're young.)

As a M/s lifestyle slave, I've seen the effects of those who sabotage relationships because they don't understand how or why we do what we do.

It comes down to the fact that not everyone will understand us; maybe they aren't supposed to understand. Maybe that's one of our challenges, our path to personal growth. So, when I hear someone say they couldn't live the way I do, I'll quietly reflect that I couldn't live the way they do; I've never thrived in a vanilla relationship. M/s is how I choose to live, and my story is different from their story. I'll kneel a little taller, knowing I've made the right choice for me.

Just as I wouldn't flourish in a vanilla life, perhaps they wouldn't prosper in a M/s relationship.

After all, we each have our own path to follow, our own trail to blaze.

Polyamory

Dan says...

Although this book is not about polyamory, we have discussed in previous writing about adding a third to our relationship. In that case, emotional connections can occur, and love can sometimes grow. So it's worth spending a bit of time on polyamory.

Polyamory, defined as "many romantic loves," is an idea (and, to some, a lifestyle) in which love and relationships are not restricted as to the number involved; relationships aren't limited to two monogamous individuals. As science fiction writer Robert Heinlein wrote: "The more you love, the more you can love, and the more intensely you love." When parents have a second child, does that dilute the love they have for their first child? Of course not. Nor do you love one more than the other (dysfunctional families aside). That kind of numerical rating system doesn't work when it comes to love. The number game for love does not work; you're not given a finite lifetime maximum or even a percentage.

Polyamory is not about cheating or about sex (although sex may be involved). One of the core concepts of polyamory is that it's approached openly and honestly. If you attend a meeting of a polyamory support or discussion group, you'll hear about the "Three Cs" of a poly lifestyle: Communicate, Communicate, and Communicate. To be even clearer, when hearts and emotions are involved, and jealousy rears its green head - it is essential to not only talk, but to listen, to hear, and to be heard. Communication is more complicated than speaking or hearing words; it's about understanding the intent, desire, motivation, and emotions behind the words.

In order for any relationship to succeed, it needs regular maintenance work. You must both/all be willing to devote the time and energy to look deeply into the relationship, assessing and addressing its growth. In poly relationships, you'll deal with the new relationship, and any insecurity within your existing relationship will come up, too. But wait, there is more! You now have a new relationship, which has created other relationships. Let's talk about a simple poly relationship, known as a "V" relationship.

In a "V" relationship, Person A maintains two somewhat separate relationships, one with Person B (the original twosome), and one with Person C. B and C are aware of each other (remember, poly is NOT a way to cheat on your partner), but they're not directly involved with each other; they're indirectly involved because what impacts A and B also impacts A and C.

There are also relationships where all three (or more) are equally involved, as well as any other combination you can imagine. Just remember that, while $1 + 1 = 2$, when you add a third person, $2 + 1$ doesn't just equal 3. Let's assume A, B, and C are a bit more intertwined. The resulting relationships could be A+B, A+C, A+B +C, or B +C. That's three individuals and many relationships.

We've seen some really interesting spider web connections, and we actually live one ourselves. At the time I'm writing this, I can be heard to say: "I was at a party with my other significant other, and we ran into her boyfriend, who was there with his wife. L asked me if I wanted to play with J, but J is involved with T; T is married to G, and my wife is dating G. So that would be complicated...and too weird!"

Here are a few things to think about; I offer them as one who's been in the trenches and stepped in a few potholes.

- Love will follow its own course. Don't try to create emotional boundaries, because emotions are unable to "feel" those boundaries.

- Don't just talk and listen; learn to hear without becoming defensive. As you listen, observe yourself and your feelings about what's being said. But LET them say what they need to say, let them feel what they need to feel. All feelings are valid.

- At the beginning of the conversation, ask "Do you just want me to listen, or is this something you/me/ we need to work on fixing?" Sometimes we just need someone to listen to us.

- Being attached to the "status quo," wanting life to be frozen in time, expecting that what was will always be...is a surefire way to get hurt. Remember, change is the only constant in life; change will occur. Believe that not all change is bad.

(Editors note: Dan & dawn went on to write the wildly popular The Polyamory Toolkit)

Polyamory and M/s

Dan says...

I am not going to tell you the right way to structure a mix of polyamory and M/s; instead, I'll tell you about my experiences. As I explored polyamory, I cut back a bit on M/s. As I explored the new outside love relationship, I treated dawn more as my peer and my friend because I wanted to be certain that being poly was truly OK with her. Did dawn have a true need to be monogamous? Did she have a want to become the poly person she believed herself to be? In that case, was her want strong enough to work at overcoming jealousy and the fear of rejection or abandonment?

I am not sure that we did it the best way, or that I really did her a favor by not being more...uhm, masterly. Today, she packs my bag when I go off to the home of my (other significant other) so she's involved in that aspect of it. And we both have external emotional relationships that have lasted over a year as of this writing. So, I suppose it worked. But if I had it to do over again...well, I might do it the same way or I might change a few things...but I suppose it would probably be a muddle of some sort, no matter what!

Musings

dawn says…

Like any couple, we had our challenges over the years. Since the beginning, our dynamic was created as a TPE; a M/s relationship. This can be a difficult style of relationship at times and about 5 years into our relationship we hit a rocky spot. We began to wonder if we could handle being Master and slave and decided to try to see if we could authentically live as a vanilla couple. This didn't last for long.

Personally, I think this 'time off' did both of us a world of good. Instead of struggling with the dynamic and maybe giving up on it totally, we gave ourselves some space and tried something else. This test reminded us of who we truly are. It brought forth our authentic selves that demanded to be allowed to survive and thrive.

These are journal writings that we published online under the titles of 'Master's Musings' and 'slave heart musings'. They show some of our struggles, and how we embraced our authentic selves and our seats of power, during a time of validation.

Slave Heart Musings, Part I

dawn says...

I know that I am slave deep in my core, deep in my heart, deep in my soul.

When we talked of becoming D/s over a decade ago, my soul sang. This is what I had been looking for, though I hadn't known what it was called. As we started with "D/s lite," I felt like I had found the real me: the me who wants to be totally owned; the me who has no secrets; the me who can let her heart and soul free, knowing they will both be cherished.

Over the years, we became more formalized, continuing to become who we are at deeper and deeper levels. My slave soul was being fed, watered, and nurtured. She was Home, and she was proud and honored to have found her Home.

For the last few years, though, and for several reasons, I tried to put her aside somewhat. Maybe I wanted to see if she was real, or maybe I wanted one more try at fitting in with those who don't understand D/s or M/s? Instead, I've found that I truly am a slave. I am my Master Dan's slave. Even while we've tried different relationship styles, I've never been able to fully suppress my slave self.

I am a slave. I have to acknowledge who I am at my core, in my heart and soul. And when Dan is my Master, my heart sings.

My Master is the man that I trust more than anyone who has ever been in my life. He is not only my Master; he is my friend, my lover, my confidant. He pushes me when I need to be pushed. He takes me when I need to be taken. He lets me fly—and he's there, waiting with open arms into which I can land safely.

As we've grown, our relationship has gone through changes, some of which pushed M/s to the side. When that happened, my heart ached to be fully His again. We've once again brought that the M/s side of ourselves to the forefront of our lives, giving it free reign. Once again I feel at peace, balanced. Slave once again has a voice, a Home. Once again, she is free, shining, singing, and embracing her power.

Master's Musings

Dan says...

A post like this has to start with an introduction and a definition or two. I am not offering the One True definition of anything, just my opinion and experience.

I began this trip some time back. Unlike many people I have met (OK, not met, but seen online), I cannot claim that at 44 years old I've been a Master for 30 years. No, my first relationships and two marriages were as vanilla as vanilla can be. It was in the year 1999 that I began a relationship that had a power exchange element to it from the get-go, and not until 2001 did a collar become a permanent part of someone's neck, someone in my charge. That's the point when I went from bedroom dom, to Dom, to Master. I did not earn my Leathers at that point. I did not get a cool scene name after serving under a powerful mentor. Instead, I claimed a slave, and the responsibilities of a Master, on a full-time, 24/7 basis. That is what defines a Master—claiming responsibility for the training, well-being, *and* actions of a slave.

My slave and I created a D/s support group and, after some time, created another. We hosted over a dozen formal events and taught an occasional class on D/s and M/s relationships.

Into the life of my first slave and me, slaves came and went. ("There have been others, to be sure. There are always others, are there not?" as Lo Pan said, in Big Trouble in Little China). But I have never been one to have more than two slaves at a time (OK, I very briefly had three); my style of training is not suited to more than a few slaves at one time. Nor are my needs so extravagant that I require five or six slaves. Each slave who came into my life brought to me and our House honor and benefit. I believe they, as well, gained something from their association with us.

At one point, I stripped my first slave of her collar, and we tried to be not-M/s. Regardless, over time, more and more M/s came into our life. No collar, no formal contract, no titles. But a slave's heart serving a Masters's desire...M/s naturally flowed back to us. Important events happen in our lives that result in realizations; we come to realize that our position of strength, our bond, is the M/s relationship we created and nurtured for so many years. We had let it become a small, subtle piece of our lives, but we are now ready to once more acknowledge and claim it.

You see, I think I had forgotten that I am a Master. I had forgotten that nearly all of my healthy relationships have been M/s ones. I fell in love with a vanilla girl (well, vanilla with a twist) and, although my relationship with my first slave continued its subtle D/s heartbeat, I began to do all right in a non-M/s relationship as well, as a non-M/s person. Fortunately, the "vanilla twist" continued to grow. Faced with new challenges, I fell back and back until I found my seat of power. My center, my core, my balance: I am a Master. And it does not change the relationship with a "vanilla twist"—I have no desire to be her Master, to change who she is, or to adjust who we are together. Our relationship is in balance as is—as long as I do not reject who I am or attempt to live in a style for which I don't have the tools. There are perhaps a thousand ways to live a polyamorous life; we are finding our path.

And this Master bows to his first slave. I bow to you, dawn, for I know how you have suffered before we became who we are. I know how you struggled to reach the place you saw you belonged. I know how you have flown free—sometimes with success, sometimes with anguish. And here you are, waiting for me to claim you once more. You are no longer in a place where you need to be claimed; you simply want to be claimed. You are waiting. You now know me better than ever; you know I will not protect you from pain, yet I will do what I can to prevent harm.

When will you come to your senses and beg for that collar?

When will I remember my honor and demand you take my collar?

Slave Heart Musings, Part II

dawn says...

Sir, I read, I cried.

Since the beginning, I have been honored to be yours....to wear your collar when it was offered and even after it was taken away. Yours I will always be, even as we explore life and different ways of living, even as we love others,

Yours I will always be.

I know deep in my core, my soul, my heart...that I am slave. Even as we attempted to live without the collar, I couldn't completely deny who I am, just as you couldn't deny who you are. That is where some of my struggle comes from; denying who I am. I am a strong person, but when I belong to you, I am empowered in ways that have always amazed me.

Sir, I bow to you, with deep honor, trust, and respect. I will always be there for you in whatever way you need me, just as you have been there for me while I've struggled with these growing pains.

I truly miss the weight of your formal collar, though you've owned me since day one. I would be truly honored to wear your collar once again. I do not 'need' your collar to be slave, for slave is who I am. But I crave your collar. I crave your ownership. I crave to do your bidding and to kneel before you as yours. I would be honored to walk this road with you as your slave. Yours

Walking–Together–Through the Dark and Back into the Light

A Contest and a Cover

Two Leather Traditions

Those two items are part of the Leather community traditions.

The Contest: The granddaddy of Leather contests is International Mr. Leather (IML), the oldest and largest gathering of Leather folk in the world. Beginning with small contests in Leather bars across the country, 12 men competed at the first IML in 1979. Held in Chicago over Memorial Day Weekend at the end of May, IML, like all the events in the Leather "contest circuit," has come a long way: IML is no longer just a hot body; he is the spokesperson for the Leather Community. IML spawned more contests than we can count, including International Ms. Leather and International Master/slave. MAsT (Masters And slaves Together), the organization for adults who live, or want to live, the Master/slave lifestyle, was founded in 1988 in San Francisco as a support organization for gay men in Master/slave relationships (MAsT is now a pansexual group). As part of MAsT, Luke Owen was instrumental in developing the International Master/slave Contest, the first relationship-based Leather title.

The Cover: there is a tradition that is making a comeback in the pansexual Leather community. This is the *presentation of a Master's cover*. This cover or cap is usually in the style of a Muir cap and is military in design, which makes sense as many of the Leather Community Traditions have their roots in the military. Another Master that is qualified in the presenting of Leather, or a group that has deemed a Master worthy of a cover by his deeds and actions usually carries out the presentation of a cover.

Why We Ran for a Master/slave Title

dawn says...

During 2008–2010, Master Dan and I went through some major changes. Because of this, our M/s dynamic grew to be stronger than ever. Because of this, we finally decided to run for Great Lakes Master/slave 2010. Great Lakes Leather Alliance was held in Indianapolis in August 2010. At another event the following month, the Ohio community rocked our world by presenting Master Dan with his Master's Cover.

Dan says...

In 2010, dawn and I competed for the Great Lakes Master and slave title, a regional title that represents 13 states. We won, which means we'll compete in February 2011, for the title of International Master and slave 2011.

The contest began on Friday morning and wrapped up on Sunday morning; it included speeches, presentations, interviews, and judging panels; we were being examined all weekend. Title contests are common in the Leather-based groups and almost non-existent in kink or non-leather-based M/s groups.

People compete and run for titles in the Leather community for a number of reasons. While it may be for "fame," it's certainly not for "fortune"! You may get some money as part of a "travel fund" to help you defray your cost to travel to the next-level competition, to promote the title at other events, etc. In the end, though, having a title will end up costing you out of pocket. You'll also spend a lot of time on your title; you'll be asked to travel, to present at events, to speechify, and to help raise funds for various organizations. Your title may even have specific requirements, such as presenting/attending X number of events during your title year and being involved in the following year's contest.

We knew the contest judges would ask us why we were running for the title. Everyone gets asked that question, and there's no right answer.

I am not by nature a competitive person. I am far more interested in being the best me I can be, preferring to compare me to myself, not to you. Competition against others always struck me as a losing proposition, since at some point you're bound to lose. No matter how great you are at whatever, someone somewhere is better. Do you only want to feel good about your accomplishments until you meet that person who's better at whatever? It makes much more sense to me to just compare myself to the guy in the mirror.

I am also not generally an ego-driven person. Titles and accolades do feel good—but fame is fleeting, and I don't want to get stuck thinking about how great something once felt. Mindfulness at the moment is what winning or losing feels like right then; it's not something on which I'm hanging my emotional hat!

So, why run? For me, it started because good friends (and previous titleholders) suggested it would be good for the community to see two individuals who were in pretty balanced emotional shape, were skilled at presenting themselves in a positive way, and had been living M/s for over ten years. We thought about that. We've presented on M/s and other topics about a dozen times each year for the last bunch of years; this title, though, would give us an opportunity to reach more people, as well as new and different audiences.

Beyond that, the big thing for me is the lack of understanding and lack of communication between the Leather and non-leather groups. Both have a lot to offer each other, but they don't often cross-pollinate; at least in the communities we have experience with. I think that comes partly from Leather-phobia and partly from miscommunication. Some in the kink community think Leather groups are still primarily focused on gay males; many in the Leather community feel that kinky folks are just swingers with floggers.

I'm most bothered when people feel they have to choose between Leather and kink, that you're either one or the other. Some people told me they assumed I would stop coming to kink events since I've become more involved in Leather events.

I want to be an ambassador, someone known to both communities and able to respond appropriately when someone expresses questions or doubts relating to either community. I want the kink community to know that the Leather community is rich in tradition and education; I want the Leather community to know the kink community has great vigor and enthusiasm. And I want to help the modern, growing M/s community to be enriched by both Leather and kink energy.

Speechless

Dan says...

For those of you who know me and were in attendance Saturday night at the 2010 COPE (Central Ohio Perversion Diversion) presented by AIS (Adventures in Sexuality), you saw something very unusual: Dan, speechless. And that doesn't often happen!

I was asked, along with my House, the power exchange tribe of House Metta, to come to the stage. There, in a ceremony led by Mollena Williams, International Ms. Leather 2010, assisted by leaders representing the Ohio community, presented my slave with a Master's Cover for me. Agreeing that I was ready, she offered the Cover to me

Speechless and with tears rolling down my cheek, I accepted the Cover, honored beyond words. As I stare at my computer right now, I am again tearfully speechless.

Being part of a community for 11 years and having them single you out for this kind of honor, is overwhelming. It's especially mind-boggling because our Ohio community doesn't have a strong element of Leather traditions. Yet, they came together, saying "Dan, you are worthy of wearing a Master's Cover." Wow. This honor did not come from judges who saw only my best face; these are the people I've known and with whom I've interacted for the full 11 years I've been an active member of the community; people with whom I've had conflicts; people who have seen my worst face; people who have seen me at my least useful point; people who've seen my most "F-—YOU!" attitude. These were the people who were patient with me as I came back around, waiting for my ego to calm down, and acknowledged we all act in the way we think best serves the community.

Of course, I am speechless. What words could possibly convey my sense of being both humbled and honored?

The only reasonable response is not one expressed in words; it is demonstrated by actions. I see this honor as a gift of responsibility; it is confirmation that thus far I have been on the right path, one that I need to continue to follow and that my behavior must reflect all the kind words that were spoken about me.

I am honored by Barak and Sheba; they put their event on the line; they took a chance; they did something that could well have blown up in their faces.

I am honored by all of you who were witnesses to the event; by those who said: "Congratulations; I know what this ceremony represents"; and perhaps even more so by those who said "Although I really have no clue about that ceremony; however, it clearly feels important to and for our community, so congratulations"; by those who were not there to witness the ceremony yet have been there for me nonetheless; and by those who have passed on but whose lives are a part of this tradition.

I express my eternal gratitude to all the slaves in my past; my slave jem, who continues to teach me how to be a better Master; Karen, my gracious and beloved significant other of three and a half years, who continues to remind me that sometimes solutions and right action can be found in a place of vulnerability with one's peers; and dawn, my slave of 11 years and my wife for nine years who put up with a newbie Master as I stumbled around and struggled with...well, everything. dawn has grown step-by-step with me, and she is every bit the reflection of who I am.

To this community, to my peers, and to my friends: I hereby commit that I will continue to serve this community to the best of my ability. I will do what I can and will offer my skills, earning this Master's Cover each and every day.

Although perhaps on occasion I will allow myself to use the honorific "Master," I remain, simply, "Dan." I charge you, my community, to remind me that the path of ego doesn't really suit me...and my fancy new Cover wouldn't fit a swelled head!

Master's Covering

dawn says...

Now that the dust has settled and Master has had a chance to process and write about what happened, I feel I can take my turn at writing about it!

Those who saw my Master's covering ceremony, understand the significance of the event not only to my Master but to the community as well. For five community members representing different Ohio groups to come together, create such a ceremony and honor Dan...it was overwhelming (which is an understatement!).

None of us were told about this. It caught us all by surprise. (I was told later that they didn't tell me because they knew I would tell Dan as I hold no secrets from him. They know me so well.) And as you may have seen, there wasn't a dry eye from those talking about Dan or from our House members that were standing up front supporting Dan.

As I stood next to Dan, the man I love, the man I've called "Master" for 11 years (though I've known him for much longer), I felt his emotional response as he listened to others describe him as a great man and a great Master, one who has matured, helped others in so many ways, and contributed to the community on so many levels. I cried as I heard and felt the love of so many people who were recognizing him for the man he is and shared that recognition with others. My heart overflowed. I know Dan does not do what he does in order to get recognition, so I know he never expected this, never guessed this would ever happen.

What they were saying about Dan couldn't have been more true. They spoke of his:

- integrity, morals, ethics, honesty, and honor;

- kindness, compassion, and passion;

- willingness to lend others his hand, shoulder, or ears;

- readiness to help others along their chosen path, be it a M/s path or some other direction;

- and presence, being there for the community on all levels: personal, local, national, and even international.

They know him so well.

My heart swelled as they talked of his commitment. And then I heard Mollena say, "We, the community leaders, believe that Dan is worthy of our respect, and this recognition. So we call dawn to join us." My heart stopped, and I slowly walked up to the stage. Why did they need me?

Mollena said: "dawn, these leaders within the Ohio community have stepped up and shown that they approve of this covering of Dan. However, the final step is in your hands. You are his slave, and you know his heart." I cried then, and

I'm crying as I write this. She continued: "If you believe that these leaders have seen the truth if you believe he is worthy of this honor, then take this Cover from my hands and cover your Master."

My heart was pounding. What could I say that would express how I felt about Him? Could my love for Him be any greater? I swallowed the lump in my throat, took a breath, and looked him in the eye; I wanted him to see how I felt about what I said and that what I was saying was the truth. I spoke to him of my love and my pride; about how we've walked this path together, not knowing how to begin but knowing we wanted a loving M/s relationship and having the commitment to follow through, to move forward.

As the words came out, feelings were racing through me. All I wanted to do was go to him, have him wrap his arms around me, hold me while I cried, and tell him how much I loved him and how proud I was of him. Instead, I took another deep breath and called to him in my traditional way. "Sir, may I," I asked as I dropped to my knees before him, before the only man for whom I've knelt. My trust and faith in him is truly immeasurable. Lacking the words to express the depth of my feelings, I simply offered Master his cover, while the tears ran down my face.

Yes, I know my Master's heart. Yes, I absolutely believe he is worthy of this honor. Yes, I offered him his Cover; it was the right thing to do, one about which my heart had not a single doubt.

Master, Dan, Sir...as your slave, and as your wife, ours has been an amazing ride. It's not always been easy as we've tried to live a life that not many people understand; we've experienced smooth sailing, struggles, growth, and changes. I can honestly say two things: one, I wouldn't have tried this with anyone else; and, two, with you I'd do it all over again. Your integrity, your honesty, and your passion for growth and living life are impressive. You have supported me in everything I do. You have helped create the person who knelt before you.

I am honored that a man such as you is my Master and husband. To you, I bow, Namaste. (Namaste means 'The Divine in me bows to the Divine in you.")

I offer thanks to everyone who made this evening so special for Dan; you are all respected leaders, all people I'm proud to call "friend." I offer thanks to everyone who made this evening so special for Dan:

- Barak and Sheba, I'm still speechless; you were smart to keep your plans secret;

- Master Owen from NLA, you have been there since the beginning for us;

- Bev from PRSCO, you're an amazing woman; and

I thank all of you: whether you watched, were part of the ceremony, warmly shook Dan's hand, or couldn't be there. To everyone: my sincerest gratitude and appreciation!!!

Our community is one in which we can all have pride!!!

Conclusion

We say...

This is, of course, not the end. At the time we are writing this, it is one day since we celebrated the 10th anniversary of our collaring and beginning a Master/slave life together. And it still feels fresh, new, exciting.

Just in the course of writing this book, we have had new experiences, challenges, and adventures. We have had to fight the urge to add 'just one more chapter'...or to start another book before the 'ink is dry' on this one.

The key to all of this, everything we have written and shared and reflected on with you is that it isn't the only way or right way or 'one true way', but our way. As we have traveled from "D/s lite" to collared to running for an M/s Leather title, we hope to have made a path clear for others to follow. Sometimes the path we have forged will be perfect for what you want to accomplish. But there will be times when the path will be yours and yours alone - and in that case, break out the machete and blaze ahead with strength and courage. It is a hard path you and we have chosen. But there simply is no other that is as fulfilling and as authentic.

We don't know what is beyond the next door...but we can't wait to find out.

Biography

From the original 2011 Edition

Dan Williams (Master Dan) has been actively engaged in the real-time M/s community for over a decade. He is the leader of the Leather tribe House Metta and is part of several M/s based groups (locally and nationally). He is also an active participant in the Recovery in the Lifestyle group, a 12-step program for those recovering from the disease of addiction and alcoholism, and has been 'clean and sober' for over 20 years. He can often be found leading RitL meetings at major events across the United States. He is proud to represent the Great Lakes region as the 2010 GLLA Master title holder.

He is also a Buddhist, a bit of a geek, and an enthusiast of live-action mock combat games.

Dawn Williams (slave dawn) is a licensed and ordained interfaith clergy and has presided over dozens of ceremonies and rituals for the alternative community. She has facilitated several spiritual and energy groups across Ohio, as well as run numerous classes on sacred sexuality. She has mentored and consulted a great number of people to assist in helping them realize their full potential. She has won a number of awards for her work, most recently Educator of the Year (PRSCO). She

happily represents the thirteen states with her Master as the GLLA slave title holder.

She has recently returned to college to earn a degree in psychology to further her passion for helping others.

Authors Note for the new edition

The above is true of us for the most part still. Since then, we've become full-time RV-ers; written 5 other books, such as expanding our power exchange writings in Hearts & Collars and on our polyamory in The Polyamory Toolkit; presented at hundreds of events; ran dozens of events ourselves; and a lot more. You can find all this and what else we are doing nowadays at www.eroticawakening.com

Also By Dan & dawn

PODCAST

The *Erotic Awakening Podcast* is the longest-running kinky polyamory power exchange podcast on the net! Join Dan & dawn every week for fun and interesting conversations! https://www.eroticawakening.com/podcast/

BOOKS

Hearts & Collars: Twenty Years in a Power Exchange Relationship

June 19, 2022

For over twenty years, Dan & dawn have been successfully engaged in a full-time loving power exchange relationship. This book recounts that journey and provides both usable tools that can apply to your relationships as well as the stories behind them.

Each chapter is presented in two views - from Dan's (power exchange leader) and dawn's (power exchange follower) perspective. After all, a book written by only 'one side of the slash' could only provide one perspective.

You'll find everything from how to get started in creating that rock-solid foundation to advanced tools for long-term growth and happiness (such as the famous Porch Time and PTE Shorthand), this is THE book for anyone seeking an emotionally connecting, long-term term and powerful power exchange relationship!

The Polyamory Toolkit: A Guidebook for Polyamorous Relationships

January 20, 2019

For nearly two decades, Dan and Dawn have navigated their journey in polyamory by being proactive, insightful and analytical. Early on, there was very little information or resources available, so the adventure required them to learn from their mistakes as well as their successes.

Each have multiple partners and have a history of polyamory relationships lasting multiple years. They have put the time and thought into creating a "toolkit" of knowledge others can implement to help their relationships survive and thrive.

Dan and Dawn write in an anecdotal, conversational style that is easy to absorb and use.

Find these and our other books at

https://www.eroticawakening.com/books/